"I've always been a big fan of Will Davis's preaching, and he writes in the same down-to-earth voice that makes you feel like you're having a heart-to-heart conversation with a friend. If you've ever been guilty of searching for *enough* in all the wrong places (ahem, like me!), I dare you to read this book. Be warned that it will make you squirm in places, but in a good way—a very good way."

—**Vicki Courtney**, author of *5 Conversations You Must Have with Your Daughter*

"I'm a Will Davis fan! I have all his books and have been impacted by his message. Succinct, empowering, and inspiring—that's the pen of Will Davis. His message of *enough* convicts me and yet causes me to see blessings through mature eyes. I'm blessed to be a blessing. Let this book take you into the deep things of God."

—**Randy Phillips** of Phillips, Craig, and Dean; lead pastor of PromiseLand Church

"I am so thankful for this book. I have been thinking about downsizing my lifestyle and freeing myself from the maintenance of too much accumulated stuff! After reading Will's book, I am convicted to actually *do* it and not think about it any longer. Simplifying my life means I can be available and ready to go when God calls me to serve and take care of his loved ones, wherever and however that might be!"

—**Nancy Turner**, host of *This Is the Day* for Moody Radio

"As usual, Will Davis Jr. has challenged me at a deep level. I am truly inspired to rethink my perspective on working, money, and the pursuit of the American dream. I highly recommend *Enough* for every American!"

—**Debbie Chavez**, talk show host at www.faithplace.org; women's conference speaker

"What can I say outside of the fact that Will's books always make me better? *Enough* gives us access to the mind and heart of an authentic Christ-follower. Clear biblical teaching, compelling illustrations, and life-impacting coaching. God spoke to me through *Enough*. I bet he'll speak to you as well."

—**Jeff Young**, spiritual development pastor at Prestonwood Church, Plano, Texas

"*Enough* challenges the status quo pursuit of the American dream, which has produced less-than-stellar results. If your goal is actually *feeling* wealthy, secure, and as though you finally have enough, then Will's book is a must-read!"

—**John Burke**, author of *No Perfect People Allowed*

Books by Will Davis Jr.

Pray Big
Pray Big for Your Marriage
Pray Big for Your Child
Faith Set Free
10 Things Jesus Never Said
Enough

ENOUGH

FINDING MORE BY LIVING WITH LESS

WILL DAVIS JR.

Revell

a division of Baker Publishing Group
Grand Rapids, Michigan

Published by Revell
a division of Baker Publishing Group
P.O. Box 6287, Grand Rapids, MI 49516-6287
www.revellbooks.com

Printed in the United States of America

Library of Congress Cataloging-in-Publication Data
Davis, Will, 1962–
      Enough : finding more by living with less / Will Davis, Jr.
         p.   cm.
      Includes bibliographical references (p.   ).
      ISBN 978-0-8007-2002-5 (pbk.)
      1. Contentment—Religious aspects—Christianity. 2. Simplicity—Religious aspects—Christianity. 3. Christian life. I. Title.
BV4647.C7D38 2012
241′.4—dc23   2012003547

Published in association with the literary agency of WordServe Literary Group, Ltd., 10152 S. Knoll Circle, Highlands Ranch, CO 80130.

The internet addresses, email addresses, and phone numbers in this book are accurate at the time of publication. They are provided as a resource. Baker Publishing Group does not endorse them or vouch for their content or permanence.

To protect the privacy of those who have shared their stories with the author, some details and names have been changed.

12   13   14   15   16   17   18   7   6   5   4   3   2   1

In keeping with biblical principles of creation stewardship, Baker Publishing Group advocates the responsible use of our natural resources. As a member of the Green Press Initiative, our company uses recycled paper when possible. The text paper of this book is composed in part of post-consumer waste.

green press
INITIATIVE

To Steve Shaver—for starting the missions revolution in my life and in our church

To Stan and Gigi Horrell—for giving me a "front-row seat" to glory

To Cecil and Ginny Campbell—for reminding me of the Bible's call on my life to serve the poor

Contents

Thanks to . . .

- Susie, Will 3, Emily, and Sara—for your nonstop encouragement, laughter, godliness, and for joining me in the pursuit of enough.
- The leaders and congregation of Austin Christian Fellowship—for loving me, supporting me, and dreaming with me.
- The wonderful people at Revell Books—for sticking with me and allowing me to write and publish *Enough*.
- Greg Johnson—for wise and godly counsel.
- David Guion—for being a friend who is closer than a brother, for modeling *enough*, and for passionately loving Jesus.
- Laura Beth Hammonds, Jackie Kincaid, and Melissa Edwards—for great food, great coffee, much laughter, and true friendship.
- Maury Buchanan and Mission Discovery—for serving the poor around the world with faithfulness and passion, and for allowing me to play along.

- Doug Ehrgott—for first introducing me to the concept of "moving toward enough."
- Todd Lewis—for saving my life on a rooftop in Mexico.
- Tony and Denise Iannitelli—*bien hecho.*
- Cory Hart—yes, you were crying.
- Bob and Gail Hughes—words cannot express . . .
- D'Ann Beck; Keith and Leanna Evans; Thom, Celia, Davis, and Anna Fulmer; Julie Grimm; Jimmy and Jeannie Hampton; Rebekah Harvey; Jeff Mandeville; Anna Mechem; Randy and Denise Phillips; Gary Sinclair; Jason and Andrea Thomas; Del and Teri Waters; Shawn Weekly; Mark Wignall; Heather Zugg—for inspiring me and making valuable contributions to this book.

Introduction

Your purpose in life isn't to make money. It isn't to live a comfortable lifestyle, to prepare for your retirement, or even to provide well for your family. Believe it or not, you're designed for something far better and much more exhilarating. If you limit your life's purpose to acquiring wealth or living comfortably, then you'll never have enough and you'll never be satisfied.

Meet Mike. From all outward appearances, he has it made. He and his beautiful family live in an affluent part of Austin. He's a Christian who loves his wife and kids and is sincerely committed to giving them the very best of everything—the best home, the best education, the best traveling experiences, the best sports and recreational opportunities, the best clothes, the best medical care—everything. As a result of that lofty goal, Mike works sixty-plus hours a week, the bulk of which he spends on the road away from home.

Recently, I caught up with Mike on one of the few days he's actually in Austin. Over breakfast tacos and coffee we talked about his goals, his frantic schedule, and his overall spiritual health. Mike confessed that he wasn't doing well. He was tired all the time and lonely on the road. He missed his wife and kids, and the relentless travel had taken a toll on their relationships, especially on his marriage. He also confessed that he and his wife were up to their ears in debt and weren't giving financially to the church, even though they knew they should be and that they were clearly living an affluent lifestyle. They simply had too much debt and overhead to be able to write checks to their church.

I asked Mike if there was any end in sight to his long workweeks, if he saw a finish line in the future where he had enough, had accomplished enough, and could back off the travel. He didn't. Then I asked him what he would have when he was at that finish line, wherever it was. "Security," he responded. I hated to burst Mike's bubble, but I had to tell him that the goal of security he was pursuing was a myth. Not only was it unattainable, but pursuing it might actually be killing the very things he was trying to protect.

It's a bit ironic, isn't it? Mike wouldn't tell you that the purpose of his life is to be rich or allow his family to live comfortably, even though he is and they do. He would tell you that he's only trying to do what God expects him to do, what any good Christian man should do—work as hard as he can and provide as much as he can for his family. He would tell you that the goals of his life are to honor God and to love his family. The ironic part is that he's working so much he simply doesn't have the time or energy to do either.

Mike is one of millions of Americans and billions of others around the world who somehow think that more matters. They've never really stopped to ask the question, "When is *enough* enough?" Maybe, at least in Western culture, it's due to our capitalistic drive. Maybe it's because our celebrity role models in government, sports, and Hollywood—and perhaps even the couple next door—all spend money like it's limitless. Or maybe it's caused by the cultural mantra that claims if we spend enough money and have enough stuff we really will find peace, prosperity, security, and happiness. It's hard to not want to try and keep up. There's only one problem—it's all a lie.

The Bible offers a better way. In the wisdom of God, the Bible includes countless verses about money and wealth, and the futility of pursuing either. The Bible teaches that it's foolish to try to satisfy the needs of a priceless, eternal human soul by throwing stuff at it. Beyond that, it tells us that we are going to be held accountable for how we manage what God has given us—specifically, our money and other resources. It tells us that we are to care for the poor, the widows, and orphans, and to help spread the hope-giving message of Jesus Christ. And it promises that there is great joy and contentment to be found in living with less, giving more, and seeking to serve others by using what God has given us. While Mike hasn't yet discovered how to have more by living with less, many others have.

Now don't panic. I'm not asking you to take a vow of poverty, and more importantly, the Bible doesn't either. I am asking you to consider the Bible's promises to those who willingly choose to live with less. I know it's counterintuitive, but the Bible actually says you'll be richer if you scale back what you have. It says your life will be fuller. You'll have less stress, more time for the things that matter, the potential for better relationships, and more joy. Bottom line: in the language of our culture, you'll be happier.

That alone is reason enough to keep reading.

Consider Tom and Kristin. Tom is a financial planner and Kristin a personal trainer. They make a good living and are successful by just about anyone's standard—beautiful kids, nice neighborhood, comfortable house, and financial security. However, as Tom and Kristin continued to grow in their discipleship, and specifically as they got involved with their church's missions ministry, they both began to sense that God wanted them to rethink their lifestyle. They came to see the disparity between how they were living, what they were modeling for their kids, and what the Scriptures taught about giving and living with *enough*.

As a result of the Spirit's leading in their lives, Tom and Kristin started making changes. They sold their house and moved into a smaller one in the same area. They increased their giving and reduced their respective workloads so they could spend more time serving. Their lives have done a complete 180-degree turn . . . and they couldn't be happier. Tom and Kristin have discovered the biblical secret of living with less. They find their hope and joy in following Jesus and in living to bless others. They have rejected the cultural notion that more matters.

In other words, they don't buy into what marketers want us to believe, the "money equals happiness" promise. Tom and Kristin are pushing back on the pressure many of us feel to spend money like there's no tomorrow, almost as if it's our duty. They don't feel obligated to keep spending money so that our nation will have a strong and thriving economy. They also understand that what they have or don't have doesn't in any way define who they are or reflect their value. They've decided to radically embrace the biblical teaching that they don't own anything—that they really are just managers of what God has entrusted to them. And they're experiencing firsthand the Bible's promises that those who live with less and give more will have all that they need—physically, spiritually, emotionally, and relationally. You can too.

Tom and Kristin are not unusual. I believe there is an *enough* revolution brewing in our culture, and I've got countless examples to prove it. A significant number of Christ-followers are coming to the conclusion that more doesn't matter and that you really can have joy, peace, and blessing by living with less. Becoming an *enough* Christian isn't as hard as it seems and not nearly as painful as your instincts may tell you. In fact, you'll be surprised at how easy it is to live with less. You'll even wonder how you got by all those years with so much. Less matters. Less really is more.

I invite you to join the *enough* revolution. In the pages that follow, you'll discover what it means to "move toward *enough*." You'll learn to recognize the myth of more and experience the joy of living with less. And you'll be gripped by the practical reality of Jesus' words: "It is more blessed to give than to receive" (Acts 20:35).

Enough Is Enough

*Give me enough food
to live on, neither too
much nor too little.*

Agur, as quoted in
Proverbs 30:8 (Message)

1

How Much Is Enough?

Enough. It's a curious word, isn't it? Why don't you say it out loud a few times—*enough, enough, enough*. I bet you can even define the word without looking it up: the condition or state of having plenty; to be full or filled; without lack. *Enough*.

We use the word *enough* many times each day without even thinking. I have *enough* gas to get home. Do you have *enough* money for the movie? We've got *enough* time for just two more questions. I don't have *enough* sugar for the recipe. We don't have *enough* money to pay our taxes. I've had just about *enough* of your back talk. I think I've got *enough* room for one more helping of cobbler.

Enough. Whatever *enough* is, we instinctively know when we do or do not have enough of it.

Except when it comes to things and money. Why is it that so many of us don't know how to define *enough* when dealing with the material and/or financial aspects of our lives? You would think that those boundaries of *enough* would be the easiest to figure out. You just define it by what you need, right? If you need $10 for a movie and you have $10, then you have *enough*. If it costs $35 to fill up your gas tank and you have $35, then you've got *enough*.

But it isn't really that simple, is it? When it comes to stuff, we wrestle with all kinds of questions about what is and isn't *enough*. How many square feet—bedrooms, bathrooms, garage, kitchen, dining room, breakfast nook, exercise room, entertainment room, workroom, and study—will make up *enough* house for us? How much car—new or used; lease or own; cloth, vinyl, or leather interior; single- or multi-CD player; V-6 or V-8 engine; GPS, speaker phone, TV, and DVD player; sun roof and/or moon roof—will be *enough* car for me? How much money—five figures (as long as the first figure is an 8 or a 9), six figures, or even seven figures—do I need to meet my needs? To feel secure? To be happy? To feel like I have *enough*? You get the point.

How can we so readily define *enough* when it comes to filling up our gas tanks but we can't define it when it comes to filling up our lives? As far as stuff is concerned, when is *enough* enough?

Beautiful Things

Victoria Frances (not her full name) believes that she was born to shop. As the editor of a Manhattan-based interior design magazine, Frances feels some sort of moral obligation to know the latest trends in home décor. Every Saturday morning Frances hits what she calls the Four B's—"Barney's,

Bendel's, Bergdorf's, and Bloomies." But her buying, as she readily admits, isn't completely job related. For more than a decade, Frances has spent thousands of dollars a week on stuff—clothes, jewelry, furniture, shoes, etc. Finding pleasure through her possessions is a key part of her sense of self-love. Frances commented, "I love to be surrounded by beautiful and exotic things."[1]

So how does Victoria Frances know when she has *enough*?

Consider Brittney and Gregg Peters, the Georgia couple who decided to sell most of their worldly possessions on eBay to cover their two kids' mounting medical expenses. After a Texas family offered them a $20,000 gift on the condition that the Peters family not sell off their possessions, Brittney and Gregg decided to downsize anyway. They chose to sell or give away most of what they had. The result was overwhelming. The Peters family was inundated with interview requests and received media coverage from all over the United States. Brittney Peters finds all the attention to be a little disheartening. She commented, "It says a lot [about] the materialistic society we live in that a family selling everything they own would make national news."[2]

How and when will the Peters family know that they have *enough*?

Lessons from Agur

How do I know when I have *enough*? Can *enough* even be quantified? Shouldn't the real definition of *enough* be left up to each person to figure out? Don't we in the United States have a constitutional right to determine our own *enough* as we pursue life, liberty, and happiness? For some, *enough* might be living in a mobile home park; for others, it might require a house in the Hamptons. Who's to say, and how can we really know?

If you're a Christian, you don't have to wonder. God knew that we would have a difficult time defining *enough*. We do well with recipes and car payments, when we know exactly how much sugar or money we need. But when it's up to us, when it comes to establishing a standard of living with *enough*, we have a hard time drawing the line.

So God gave us a standard. His Word offers us several clear and, I might add, simple definitions of *enough*. The bad news is that God's definition of *enough* and mine don't typically line up. I'm afraid that God's *enough* is much less than my *enough*.

Let's begin in Proverbs—the Old Testament book of wisdom. Written and/or edited mostly by Solomon, the Proverbs also contain a few sayings offered by relatively obscure biblical characters. One such character is Agur, the son of Jakeh. I'm sure his name rings a bell. I mean, he's right up there with Moses, David, and Paul. I'm sure you're thinking, "Oh yeah, Agur son of Jakeh. He's one of my favorite biblical writers!"

Thirty-three verses—that's Agur's entire contribution to the Old Testament. Not really what I'd call a biblical heavy hitter. But what Agur lacks in verbosity he makes up for in veracity. His words pack quite a punch, and it's the obscure Agur who offers us our first real biblical definition of *enough*. Here's what he wrote:

O God, I beg two favors from you; let me have them before I die. First, help me never to tell a lie. Second, give me neither poverty nor riches! Give me just enough to satisfy my needs.

For if I grow rich, I may deny you and say, "Who is the LORD?"
And if I am too poor, I may steal and thus insult God's holy
name. (Prov. 30:7–9 NLT)

Since this isn't a book on truth telling, I'll skip Agur's first
request. It's his second petition that speaks so poignantly to
our topic of *enough*. Agur must have been a very wise man.
He had the sense to pray not only that he wouldn't live in
poverty—poverty is a terrible condition for any human to
endure—but also that he wouldn't be rich. That's where he
loses me. I can honestly confess that I've never prayed that
I wouldn't be rich. I mean, how can you seriously not want
to be rich? Isn't that the great American dream? Isn't that
the secret of happiness? Doesn't money guarantee security
and comfort? No, at least not according to Agur. And you
can bet that as a king, he'd been around the block a few
times. He'd probably had up-close looks at both poverty
and riches.

What does Agur pray for? In a word, *enough*. In a phrase,
"just enough to satisfy my needs." And that begs the first
million-dollar question, doesn't it? What do I need?

Daily Bread

"What do I need?" If you can figure that one out, you can skip
the rest of the book and move on to much lighter subjects.
I need food. I need air. I need water. But I also need clothes.
I need a place to live. I need income. I need transportation.
So what do I really *need*? And when does *need* move over
into the much more exciting world of *want*? I need food,
but I want pizza. I need water, but I want it to be from the

Rockies, or at least from an Arkansas spring. I need clothes, but I want Levi's jeans and Ariat boots. On and on it goes. That's why we have such a difficult time defining *enough*. In the increasingly gray area between wants and needs, finding *enough* can prove to be very elusive.

Enter Jesus. The man we worship as King of Kings and Lord of Lords never struggled with the concept of *enough*. The God who left heaven to live as a slave, the King of the universe who had no earthly place to lay his head, the Creator of all things who died with absolutely nothing, never once struggled to figure out what *enough* meant. And he didn't hesitate to make the meaning clear to his disciples.

When the disciples asked him to teach them to pray, Jesus gave them the brief yet profound model of the Lord's Prayer. In it, he included a line about seeking God's provision. I'm sure you can quote it: "Give us this day our daily bread" (Matt. 6:11). In one sweeping statement, Jesus presented his followers with a clear picture of what he considered to be *enough*. Jesus' daily bread reference no doubt harkens back to the account of Israel's wanderings in the wilderness, where God gave them daily provision of manna and quail for forty years.

In Jesus' mind, that's all God promises. He promises to give us what we need today. He doesn't promise to provide for tomorrow, next week, next month, or next year. He doesn't promise to provide in advance for our retirement. All he offers is today. According to God, today is all you need. And you know what's really interesting? If we lived on what Jesus says is *enough*, if we lived with just *enough* to meet our immediate needs, most of us would think we were poor. But we wouldn't be. We'd simply have *enough*.

Traveling Light

Under the obvious direction of the Holy Spirit, the apostle Paul also chimed in on the discussion of *enough*. In his first letter to his young disciple Timothy, Paul offered a series of teachings to those who were wealthy. At the end of his teaching, Paul shared his own understanding of *enough*. He wrote, "If we have food and clothing, we will be content with that" (1 Tim. 6:8).

Really? Food and clothing? That's not a lot to live on. Where's the big screen TV? Where are my electronic gadgets? Where's my retirement plan? Paul wasn't saying that these things are bad, just that they aren't necessary. Paul added a new word to our working definition of *enough*—contentment. By doing so, he lowered the bar dramatically on what the Bible says we need—food and covering. Basically, if we have food in our stomachs, clothes on our backs, and a roof over our heads, we're good.

Can you see the obvious tension that exists between how so many of us live and what the Bible says is really necessary? Do you see the great distance between how our culture defines *enough* and how Agur, Jesus, and Paul defined it? What do we do with that? Are we sinning because we have savings accounts? Am I out of God's will because I live in more than a one-bedroom house? And what if you don't feel content with just food and clothing? What if you think you need more? What do you do then?

Top Ten Benefits of Living with Enough

Before we answer those questions, let's think about some of the advantages of living with *enough*. How can mere daily provisions really be better than surplus? Why shouldn't we want a little more of what we have? For folks like you and me, who most likely will never be really rich by our culture's standards, but who know that having a little more money in the bank would be very helpful when paying bills, a life with *more than enough* can sound downright dreamy.

So why downsize? Why scale back? Why pray for *just enough* like Agur did? Let me state the question in a more contemporary way: If you choose to pursue the elusive concept of *enough*, if you limit how you live and what you spend, what's in it for you? Why should you and I embrace the radical lifestyle of living with less? Here are ten great reasons to live with *enough*:

1. *You'll have more time.* Stuff and money require managing. Things break or need cleaning or dusting or servicing or upgrading. Money requires management. It has to be invested and reinvested. And all of that takes time. The irony of having more is that when you finally get what you think you want, you still won't be satisfied. And your "stuff" will cause you to spend more of what you can't get back—time.

2. *You'll have more peace.* Curiously, having *more than enough* rarely brings more peace. Money can't shield you from cancer and wealth can't prevent a miscarriage. Living in a nice house or driving a new car won't make your marriage better. In fact, having *more than enough* often increases your stress and distracts you from the things in life that really matter—pursuing God and loving the people he has placed in your life.

3. *You'll help your relationships.* Living with *enough* will actually help your relational world. You'll have more

time and emotional energy to invest in your loved ones and even in those friends, neighbors, and co-workers whom God might be calling you to serve. Think about it—if wealth and material comfort really brought happiness, then nations that enjoy prosperity ought to have the healthiest relationships on the planet. We all know better. Couples with six-figure incomes typically have the same or higher divorce rates and the same relational difficulties as those with smaller incomes. Susie and I have watched our income increase dramatically over the last twenty years, but it hasn't helped our marriage one iota. If anything, our increased earnings have increased our stress and conflict.

4. *You'll be more content.* Are you tired of trying to keep up with the Joneses? (By the way, have you ever talked to the Joneses? They're not content either. If they were, they wouldn't need to be kept up with. Think about it.) If you're in the habit of collecting, chasing, pursuing, and admiring more stuff, then there is always going to be something else you want. There will always be something messing with your contentment. But when you declare that you have *enough*, suddenly contentment will become much more second nature to you. When you stop looking, stop longing, and stop lusting for other things, you set yourself up to be much more at peace with where you are in life and with what you have.

5. *You'll have less or no debt.* If you stop spending money on stuff, you'll have less debt and eventually will be debt free. If you're not buying things and spending money all the time, you'll have the cash reserves necessary to

fix the broken dishwasher, replace the dead hot water heater, or even handle the college tuition for the kids. Less spending means less debt, and less debt means less stress.

6. *You'll be prepared for tough financial times.* I'm writing this the day after the US stock market took another five-hundred-point dive. Other markets around the world took similar hits. I don't know what your economy will be like when you read this, but I do know that world economies are going to ebb and flow. Natural disasters, war, poor leadership, and other economic factors are going to cause the values of our respective currencies to wax and wane. Interest rates are going to climb, gas prices will increase, the cost of goods and services will go up, and then—maybe—they'll come back down. You do not want to be in debt and have significant financial overhead when those difficult days come calling. The big house, the nice car, or the time-share in Aspen might become the albatross around your neck that wrecks your marriage or keeps you from being able to retire when you want to. But if you're living with *enough*, you're much more likely to have the financial means to navigate those difficult times.

7. *You'll be better equipped to respond to need.* Even though Israel was a homeless group of former slaves for over forty years, God still expected them to care for the poor and needy among them. He expects the same of us. But curiously and tragically, having wealth doesn't typically increase one's benevolence. Statistics still show that the most generous people among us are those who have less, not more. If you're waiting until

you hit a certain level of income before you start giving or helping others, stop waiting. God wants you to enjoy the fruits and joys of helping others right now. He wants you to be like Joseph and the Egyptians when the seven-year famine hit. Not only will you have what you need, but you'll be in a position to help others as well.

8. *Your life will be simpler.* The Bible clearly affirms the value of simple living. As we've already seen, simplicity reduces stress and enhances relationships. It helps you focus on what matters and gives you the discernment to reject what doesn't. But the more complex your lifestyle becomes—specifically, the more material and financial overhead you have—the less simplicity you'll enjoy. Simplicity and stress have an inverse relationship: the more you have of the former, the less you'll have of the latter.

9. *You'll have better intimacy with God.* If living with *enough* breeds simplicity, and simplicity helps our relationships, then it stands to reason that living with *enough* will help our relationship with God as well. Actually, simplicity enhances spirituality; it creates an environment in which your relationship with God can thrive. That's why monks and others seeking to know more of God don't retreat to the Hamptons or Beverly Hills; they go to the desert. Riches and material things are spiritual distractions. They divert our attention not just from God but from spiritual matters entirely. Living with more sets your focus on earthly, material matters, and it's nearly impossible to grow spiritually when you've got your eyes on temporal things.

10. *You'll have more joy.* This is by far the best reason to embrace living with *enough*. Joy has nothing to do with circumstances, but it has everything to do with perspective. If riches brought joy (or even happiness), then those of us with *more than enough* would be the most joyous people on earth. If riches brought joy, then King Solomon (one of the wealthiest men in history) wouldn't have lamented in Ecclesiastes about the meaninglessness of his life. But the reality is that riches often sap the joy right out of us. They're a cheap substitute for the spiritual, soul-satisfying treasure of a life of intimacy with God. When Jesus promised to give us abundant life, he wasn't talking about wealth. If that were the case, he wouldn't have died for us; he could have just written each of us a check. Jesus' death shows us that what we need most is access to God, and that's something riches can never give us. Joy can't be bought, but it can be snuffed out. Joy thrives best in an environment of less, not more.

Moving Toward Enough

From Melissa: As a single mom, simplicity is key for me. The idea of "less is more" is my way of life. I only buy used cars, which keeps my budget manageable—NO CAR PAYMENTS! Also I recently did a complete overhaul of my housing and downsized dramatically. It has been such a huge relief and has helped me see how I can be more efficient when I go shopping and in how I organize my life. My budget is simple: rent, electricity, phone, car insurance, child care, gas, food—like I said, simple! Keeping it simple takes a lot of stress out of life for me. I am much better equipped to deal with life's curveballs. For me it is really about knowing that all I have comes from God, and taking care of what he has given me is really important. It is the least I can do.

For Further Reflection

1. Read Matthew 6:11 seven times. Each time you read it, emphasize and reflect on the significance of one word (GIVE us this day; Give US this day; Give us THIS day; etc.).
2. Read Philippians 4:11–12 and think about how much Paul's statement does or does not reflect how you feel.
3. Considering where you are in your life right now (marriage and/or family, career, housing, retirement plans, etc.), how close are you to being able to declare that you have *enough*?

2

The Oldest Trick in the Book

content (adj.): fulfilled or satisfied
Examples:
1. The baby looks *content* in her crib.
2. A fancy hotel is not necessary; I'd be *content* with a warm meal and a clean place to sleep.
3. No, I don't want to play. I'm *content* to watch.
4. Not *content* to stay at home, she set off to see the world at the age of sixteen.
5. Polls show that voters are growing less and less *content* with the current administration.

Maui

Imagine with me for a minute that you live on the island of Maui—alone. Okay, maybe you live there with your spouse or your best friend. But no one else. And imagine that you have the entire island for your own personal enjoyment. Let me put that into perspective for you.

Maui is the second largest of the Hawaiian Islands, with a total land area of 729 square miles. It is 48 miles long and 26 miles across at its widest point. The magnificent Haleakala Volcano (now dormant) soars to 10,023 feet above sea level. Imagine all those green jungles, all the pristine beaches and mountain slopes, all the waterfalls, caves, and unexplored terrain—and it's all yours. It's yours to enjoy, to play in, to cultivate, and to call home. With only one small exception. Imagine that on the island of Maui there is a very dangerous section that's only 10' by 10'. It's one hundred square feet of trouble waiting to happen. It's beautiful; in fact, it's probably the most beautiful place on the entire island. It's attractive but still deadly. The area is clearly marked with signs and fences warning you to stay out and clearly communicating the risks if you don't.

You get the picture? You've got 729 square miles to play in, minus one very small 10' x 10' section. Question: could you stay out of it? Would you be content with the 728.99999 square miles of unlimited Maui, or would your curiosity and desire for more get the best of you and drive you to the turf that is off-limits?

That's basically the situation Adam and Eve faced in Genesis 3. When the Bible says they were in a garden, please don't make the mistake of thinking about the kind of garden you might have in your yard. This was a wild, beautiful, vibrant, and very large region, and its beauty would have surpassed anything we have on earth today. Honestly, we can't imagine the scope of the beauty and grandeur of what Eden would have been. And Adam and Eve had the place to themselves.

They could run, frolic, play, live, eat, and sleep to their hearts' content in this paradise. Nothing was off-limits—except one tree. One tree, that's all. "Don't touch the tree in the middle of the garden." That was the rule—the only rule—that they had to abide by.

Could you have done it? If God turned you loose in a Maui-sized playground and told you to stay away from just one tree, could you have obeyed him? You would think that with all the other options Adam and Eve had, keeping that one rule wouldn't have been a problem. But you probably know the end of the story, and it isn't pretty. They violated God's one rule, did the very thing he asked them not to do, and we've all been paying for it ever since. The really bad news is that if you and I had been there, we would have done the same thing. In fact, we're still doing it today.

All Dressed Up with No Place to Go

Greg and Gretchen were making a lot of progress. It was Greg's second marriage, Gretchen's first. After a bit of a bumpy start, they seemed to have turned a corner. They were learning to communicate better, learning to encourage and support each other, and were actually starting to have fun together. Beyond that, two really great things had happened: God had given them two beautiful daughters, and they had started going to church. Both Greg and Gretchen had been raised in the church, but they had fallen away from their faith in college as so many of us do. When the kids came along, they decided they needed all the parenting help they could get, and the local church seemed like a great place to find it. It worked. They were growing in their faith and really enjoying being a family. They appeared, by God's grace, to be over the hump in their marriage.

And then something terrible happened. Greg started making more money—a lot more. His annual income went from the high five figures to the mid six figures. Now, I don't mean that it's terrible to make a lot of money, but I do mean that if you're not equipped to handle it, money can be devastating in a relationship. Along with Greg's new success came the usual trappings: the country club membership; the private school for the kids; longer, more frequent, and more expensive vacations; and, of course, the new house.

Gretchen had always dreamed of having a large, country-style home on a lake. With Greg's new income, they would finally be able to build their dream home. So they bought one and a half acres of land with one hundred feet of waterfront on a beautiful lake in their hometown. They drew up plans for a six-thousand-square-foot home that was bound to grace the cover of architecture and lifestyle magazines around the country.

And then they started fighting. Gretchen and Greg fought about everything related to the house—the color of the tile, the type of landscaping, the size of the bedrooms, the shape of the pool, the type of marble in the bathrooms and granite in the kitchen, whether to have a two- or three-car garage, and of course, the price.

To be honest, Greg resented the whole thing. He loved Gretchen and wanted to give her the house of her dreams, but he also felt pressured to work longer hours to keep up with Gretchen's tastes. He would have been just as happy living in their current home. Now the conflict and stress of the new home were really taking a toll on him.

By the time Gretchen and Greg were able to finally move into their new "dream home," their marriage was a nightmare. They were barely speaking, had very little romance, and both were finding comfort in other sources, some that weren't so healthy. The girls had obviously sensed the tension, and it was starting to wear on them as well.

Gretchen and Greg had their dream home. They were indeed the talk of the town. But their future was uncertain. Neither was sure if the other would still be living in their dream home in a year.

I wish I could tell you that the above story was fictional, but it's not. I've changed the names and a few details, but I've seen the same story played out more times than I can remember. It seems that we really are still falling for the deceitful allure of more.

Meanwhile, Back in the Garden

Have you ever wondered what trick Adam and Eve fell for? I mean, what exactly was the temptation? What was the bait they took? In a word, it was *contentment*; or rather, the lack of it. Here's the text from Genesis 3:

> Now the serpent was more crafty than any of the wild animals the LORD God had made. He said to the woman, "Did God really say, 'You must not eat from any tree in the garden'?" The woman said to the serpent, "We may eat fruit from the trees in the garden, but God did say, 'You must not eat fruit from the tree that is in the middle of the garden, and you must not touch it, or you will die.'" "You will not surely die," the serpent said to the woman. "For God knows that when you eat of it your eyes will be opened, and you will be like God,

knowing good and evil." When the woman saw that the fruit of the tree was good for food and pleasing to the eye, and also desirable for gaining wisdom, she took some and ate it. She also gave some to her husband, who was with her, and he ate it. (Gen. 3:1–6)

The first thing the serpent did was to call into question the goodness of God and his provision for Adam and Eve. It's the oldest trick in the book, literally. Never mind that God had created an entire heavenly playground just for them, he was still mean. He was keeping something from them. He was withholding. Why would God do that? Didn't he want them to be happy? Why would he keep such a beautiful tree from people he claimed to love?

At the heart of this attack on God's character was also an attack on the nature of his provision for Adam and Eve. Satan attacked their contentment. Now get this: Satan lured these first two humans by tempting them to take their eyes off of what God *had* given them and to focus on what he *hadn't*. That's the root of discontentment. You stop focusing on what God has done and start looking at what he hasn't done (or at what you think he hasn't done). And when you do, when you start longing for what you don't have, you run the risk of losing everything.

It's this age-old temptation that causes a man or woman to betray his or her spouse and have an affair. It's this same temptation that entices couples to uproot from family, friends, church, and community and move across the country, all in the name of making more money. And it's this same lie of the devil that leads men and women to work a ridiculous number of hours a week in the pursuit of something that, once they get it, only sets them up to want something else. It never ends. Satisfaction never comes.

When Adam and Eve ate from the forbidden tree, not only did they not get what Satan promised (remember, all he does is lie), they lost what they had. They lost the garden and their unique status with God—all in the name of having more.

What have you lost, or what do you risk losing, in the name of getting that next thing? Have you bought the lie that it's not what you have but what you don't have that will really satisfy you? Discontentedness calls into question the very character and provision of God. It's basically open rebellion before God. Don't fall for it.

Moving Toward Enough

If it's not broken, don't fix it. We spend millions of dollars each year just updating our houses. We repaint the kitchen or recover the couch or buy a larger television, and we typically do so when there's nothing really wrong with the kitchen, the couch, or the TV. Instead of spending the money on what isn't really broken, why not put it in savings and live with a somewhat dated couch? Or better yet, buy a new couch for someone who needs one. We can take major steps toward *enough* simply by not fixing things that aren't broken.

For Further Reflection

1. Read Exodus 20:17 and think about areas of your life where you might be coveting what someone else has.
2. Read 1 John 2:15–17: "Do not love the world or anything in the world. If anyone loves the world, the love of the Father is not in him. For everything in the world— the cravings of sinful man, the lust of his eyes and the

boasting of what he has and does—comes not from the Father but from the world. The world and its desires pass away, but the man who does the will of God lives forever." Now define "the cravings of sinful man," "the lust of his eyes," and "the boasting of what he has and does" in your own words.

3. Why do you think John said that you can't love the world and God at the same time?

3

Finding Your Enough

When my son Will was very young—probably about eighteen months—we made the daring decision to take him with us to dinner at a nice restaurant. We were on vacation and thought it would be great to treat ourselves to a dinner that didn't come out of a box. And for some reason, we thought our active eighteen-month-old would cooperate.

I remember sitting at the restaurant and reading the menu while visions of steak and lobster danced in my head. Will was munching on a relish tray the waiter had set out as an appetizer. About the time Susie and I were set to order our scrumptious meal, Will pushed up in his high chair and announced in toddler-speak, "Aoul doe!" (read, "All done!"). We were done indeed. There was no chance of getting that kid to sit there long enough for us to order, much less wait for and then eat our gourmet meal. He was done and so were we.

What does it take to push back from the table and declare, "All done!" To decide that we have *enough*? Let's find out together.

Concepcion

Concepcion was a lively, passionate Christ-follower who lived on a small piece of land in an area outside of Managua known as La Luz. In her late sixties, Concepcion lived with her children and grandchildren on a high point overlooking the city. But for all the beauty of her surroundings, Concepcion's living conditions were anything but beautiful. Her "house" was built out of old, rotting wood pieces, cardboard, and some scrap sheet metal. It was the size of a small garage and was built on an incline. Whenever it rained, water ran through Concepcion's house, making a muddy mess of everything. Concepcion slept on the ground on cardboard sheets because of her bad back. Like most people in poverty, she lived day-to-day, meal-to-meal. She was also extremely generous.

Concepcion's house was home to far more people than it was suited for (actually, it wasn't suited for any person). At night, adults and children crammed into the little shelter. She just couldn't say no to others in need. But her giving went beyond that. Concepcion knew how powerfully Jesus' message gives hope and transforms lives, even in the darkest of settings. She also knew that having a strong church nearby was critical to developing and growing faith. She wanted her kids and grandchildren to know the same hope that she did and to have a neighborhood church home that could encourage them (something she never had). So Concepcion did a radical thing. She gave most of her land to a local pastor and asked that a church be built on it to serve the people of La Luz.

Let me try to put some perspective on that. That land was all she had to her name. It amounted to less than a quarter acre, but it was probably worth a small fortune to Concepcion. An equivalent for you or me would be our giving away an expensive tract of land—one that could have brought us significant financial reward. Actually, that's not an accurate parallel. If we gave a tract of land, chances are we'd still have more left over. Concepcion didn't. That land was all she had—and she gave it away so a church could be built there.

What kind of mind-set drives a person to do such a thing? What kind of person gives away land? I know several savvy Christian businessmen, and few if any would ever just give away something like that. There's always a view to the return on investment. There's always a cost-benefit analysis. And there's always the temptation to use the resource for something more profitable.

So what was behind Concepcion's giving? Was she naïve? Was she irresponsible? Should she have used that land to benefit her family? What makes a person do such a thing?

Pushing Back from the Table

How do you know when you have *enough*? What does it take to call "All done!" in the pursuit of more, to push back from the table and determine that your cup is full? With college tuition, car payments, kids' weddings, or an uncertain economy still looming in the future, how can we possibly ever get to the point of really having *enough*? Beyond that, our society thrives on spending; it's what drives our economy. Isn't it downright unpatriotic to not support our economy by deciding we have *enough*? How do you really know where to draw the line, and then how do you have the courage to draw it?

The good news is that determining your level of *enough* isn't complicated at all. And once you figure out what your *enough* is, you'll be amazed at how free you'll feel. Here is a simple four-step process you can use to find and stay at your level of *enough*:

1. *Take a look around.* Pause a minute to take in all that you have. Look at where you live—home, furniture, cars, appliances, clothes, and electronics. Think about your accounts—savings, 401(k), checking, stocks and bonds, etc. As best you can, take a mental survey of everything you have, whether it's a lot or a little. Got it? Now go to step 2.

2. *Say this out loud: "I have enough."* That's right—you have *enough*—today, right now, regardless of your circumstances, you have *enough*. Say it again, "I have *enough*." The truth is, you probably have *more than enough*. There may be things you want—things you'd like to have—but most of us really don't need much else. And that's true whether you're rich or poor, whether you have a ton of savings or none. It's true today whether you are employed or unemployed, retired or just starting out in your first job. It's true whether you're paid hourly, by the job, or salaried. I know that you may not feel like you have *enough*, and I fully understand what that's like. When Susie and I look at trying to pay off one set of student loans, with one kid about to graduate from college and another just about to start,

I don't have a clue how we're going to do it. But that doesn't change our reality. We have *enough*. And so do you. Want to say it again? "I have *enough*." Okay, now go to step 3.

3. *Look unto the hills.* I'll keep this one brief, as I will say more about it later on. Step 3 is about reminding ourselves of the source of our hope and provision. David wrote, "I lift up my eyes to the hills—where does my help come from? My help comes from the LORD, the Maker of heaven and earth" (Ps. 121:1–2). We tend to panic when we don't know how we're going to pay tomorrow's bills or put food on the table. We worry about retirement and our kids' future. But the Bible reminds us that our hope has never been in what we can produce—in our jobs, our bank accounts, our retirement funds, Wall Street, or the government. Our hope, future, and promise are all in God. That's how you know you have *enough*; because whatever God has, you have. You may not see it today, but it will be there when you need it. To use the words of Paul, let's set our hearts on things above, where Christ is seated at the right hand of God, and set our minds on things above, not on earthly things (see Col. 3:1–2). Now, let's go to step 4.

4. *Find a need and meet it.* One of the best ways to recognize your own *enough* is to see the *less than enough* of someone else. I am much less likely to want those new jeans or to think I "need" that new wrench set if I'm aware of the hand-to-mouth existence of my neighbor just down the street. It's amazing how much perspective can be gained by just taking our eyes off ourselves and

looking at the plight of others. If you'll get in the habit of seeing your stuff—money, home, resources, and so forth—as the possible solution to someone else's problems or the answer to someone else's prayers, then you'll be well on your way to embracing and even celebrating your *enough*.

The Thirty-Second Test

On Sunday, September 4, 2011, a series of devastating wildfires broke out across central Texas. Strong winds and the already drought-stricken landscape made for a perfect storm of wildfires that had plenty of fuel to burn uncontrollably for the better part of a week. At one point during the week, over sixty fires were burning statewide. The loss of life, property, and homes was more than most of us who live in the area could get our brains around. It was a tragic first for central Texas.

Twenty-three homes were lost in the affluent Steiner Ranch area just west of our church. Two families in our church completely lost their homes, and several others in our church had their homes badly damaged by the fires. Residents in Steiner and the other areas only had a few minutes of warning before they were forced to flee the approaching flames. Some had less than a minute. They had to grab what they could and then run for their lives.

The first night of the fires, our church parking lot and a nearby high school gym were filled with hundreds of adults, children, and pets, many smelling like smoke. Some families didn't even have time to get their pets. They escaped with their loved ones and the clothes on their backs.

So ask yourself—if you only had thirty seconds to grab whatever you could in your home before it was burned to the ground by fire, what would you take? When you answer that question you'll be right at the center of what having *enough* really means.

Right Here, Right Now

There is an additional mind-set that exists among those who have decided they have *enough*. It's what drives people like Concepcion to release what they have for the benefit of others, even when conventional wisdom says they shouldn't. I call it the "right here, right now" (RHRN) mind-set. RHRN thinking is fueled by the belief that God is always at work around us and that every moment is ripe with opportunity to join in his kingdom work. It asserts that God is doing something eternal right here and right now. Forget tomorrow, forget next Sunday—just seize the here and now opportunities that God gives us. In John 5:17 Jesus commented, "My Father is always at his work to this very day, and I too am working." Jesus epitomized the RHRN attitude. He didn't limit his kingdom work to when he was in a synagogue or the temple. He rather chose the moment-to-moment approach to look for chances to promote his Father's work. As a result, we read about his teaching and miracles being done on hillsides and during fishing trips, at funerals and parties, and even in his daily travels. Wherever he went, he worked. He never worried about what was going to happen the next day or if he would have provisions. He just met others' needs and let God take care of his own.

So can we. Those with an RHRN mind-set look for opportunities in the details of their daily lives to align themselves with God's kingdom work. RHRN thinkers also believe that their possessions and time are at the beck and call of God. They believe that if there are needs around them that they feel led to meet, then they can release their resources right then and there to meet those needs and still have the full assurance that God can and will replenish what they have given away. Such thinking is what led Concepcion to give her land to a church and what leads people like you and me to release our resources for God's kingdom causes every day.

By the way, I preached recently at the church in La Luz, right next to Concepcion's home. It was overflowing with smiling, worshiping, and desperately needy men, women, and children. Concepcion wasn't there; she's in heaven now. But her daughter and grandchildren were there, and her legacy lives on.

Moving Toward Enough

Practice the one-year rule. At least once a year, go through your closets. Take out anything—clothes, shoes, hats, ties, whatever—that you haven't worn in a year and give it away. If you haven't used it in the past 365 days, you don't need it. Do the same in your garage, kitchen, basement, and attic. If you have stuff that's just sitting there, especially stuff that someone else could use, get rid of it.

For Further Reflection

1. Read Acts 4:32–37. What do you think makes a believer act like Concepcion or Barnabas did?

2. Read John 5:17–19. How can you start to develop a moment-to-moment awareness of what God is doing around you?

3. Think about your day today. How might it have been different if you had approached it with a "right here, right now" mind-set?

More Than Enough

I tell you the truth, it is hard for a rich man to enter the kingdom of heaven.

Jesus, as quoted
in Matthew 19:23

4

Perspective

More than enough. If *enough* means to have plenty, then what does it mean to have *more than enough*? I guess it means that we have more than plenty, more than what is sufficient, more than we need.

Agur said that he only wanted *enough* to meet his needs. So would he define *more than enough* as having more than he needed? Jesus said that *enough* was having daily bread. If we have bread that will last a week or a month, is that *more than enough* bread? If we have money saved for retirement or a rainy day fund, does that mean we have *more than enough* money? Paul said that *enough* meant to have food and covering, so can we assume that if we have more than mere food and covering, we have *more than enough*? And if we do, so what?

Is it wrong to have more than just the bare minimum that life requires? Does God really want us to live day-to-day and hand-to-mouth? Surely that can't be what he intends? And if he does expect us to live that way, why does he give many of us more than we need? If we're not supposed to have *more than enough*, why does he give it to us?

Ambushed

I grew up rich; I just didn't know it at the time.

My father grew up in a single-parent household. He and his mother were poor. For my father, provision was a great way to show love. He figured that if he could give his family what he never had, he'd be a pretty successful dad. So he worked long and hard to make sure we had every opportunity a family could have. For that I'm very grateful.

I've never known what it is to want or lack for anything, not even close. In reality, I lived a very cushy life growing up: ski trips at Christmas and spring break, my own bedroom and bathroom in a nice house in an affluent part of town, long family trips in the summer, new clothes, new cars, a summer house on the lake, complete with ski boat, and world-class educational opportunities. I don't think these things spoiled me, but I do believe they numbed me to the reality of how people live who aren't so financially favored. I graduated from college, went on to graduate school, and then became a pastor without ever really coming face-to-face with poverty or suffering. But God would soon change that.

In the summer of 2002, I took a much-needed sabbatical from my job as a pastor. My church was gracious enough to give me eight weeks off and my wife was gracious enough to allow me to spend much of that time hiking in the Rockies with our son. We spent several weeks climbing fourteen-thousand-foot mountains in Colorado.

In the next-to-last week of my break, I agreed to accompany my daughter and several other kids in our student ministry to Reynosa, Mexico, with a ministry called Mission Discovery. Mission Discovery (missiondiscovery.com) is a Nashville-based ministry that builds homes for the impoverished and supports orphanages in Mexico, Africa, Jamaica, the Dominican Republic, Haiti, and the United States. Our job was to build a small one-room home (it's about the size of a small storage shed that you might have in your backyard, without electricity or running water) for a family. Reynosa is just south of the Texas/Mexico border and is the final stop for thousands of families trying to work their way north into the United States. Because most of them are unable or unwilling to enter the United States illegally, and because most are desperately poor, they are forced to create makeshift shelters out of anything they can find. Some families or groups of families live in those pitiful dwellings for years. It's hard to imagine, but the little cubicles we build for these people improve their living conditions exponentially.

This is embarrassing to admit, but that trip was my first real missions experience. I was a church leader and had been a Christian for over thirty years, but I had never personally been involved in any form of missions. As a result, I really didn't know what to expect and I certainly wasn't looking forward to the trip. I was going to support my daughter and our student ministry, not because I had any sense of responsibility to serve the people in Reynosa.

In short, I got ambushed. It was without question the best week of my sabbatical. Don't get me wrong; this was no easy or restful week. The temperatures were well over a hundred degrees each day on the work site, and we had to drive over an hour each way, including crossing the United States/Mexico border just to get there. But what I saw, heard, smelled, and felt changed me. It broke me and marked me for the rest of my life.

I had never before looked directly into the face of poverty. I had never stared into the eyes of a widow who was uncertain if she could feed her kids the next day. I had never seen children running about and playing in the dirt roads of the *colonia* in their underwear, simply because they had no other clothing. I had never seen a special needs child roaming the streets alone like an abandoned pet because her parents could no longer care for her. And I had never seen men, stripped of all sense of dignity and self-worth because of the generational ravages of poverty, use drinking and sex (actually *rape* would be a better word) as a means of passing the time. I had never seen any of that before.

What I saw made me angry. That's a common emotion for many people who experience poverty for the first time. I got mad and was even a little ashamed of how I'd lived with such wealth and such waste. I probably throw away more food in a year than some of those people will consume in a lifetime. I was mad at the disparity that existed between them and me. Here they were, just a few hours' drive from my back door, and yet our worlds couldn't have been farther apart.

What do we do with that? How do I justify the inequity? Should I feel guilty because I was blessed to be born in the United States where life and opportunities are so much different from theirs? And where was God in all this? How could he sit quietly by while so many people suffered just a few hours away from so many who had so much? I didn't have the answers to these troubling questions, and I ended up just being angry and frustrated.

But if I'm honest, my anger isn't what marked me the most. It was the joy of the people whom we served. Rarely in my life had I seen such high levels of passion for Christ and sheer, unadulterated joy. Many of these people had deep, profound relationships with Jesus. They didn't feel overlooked or abandoned by him. That's what got me the most. In the face of such terrible living conditions and such chronic suffering, they had levels of faith that humbled me.

There I was, the rich gringo who was there to help them, and yet I was the one who felt poor. I was the one who didn't seem to get it. From an earthly, material standpoint, I had everything and they had nothing. But from the standpoint of God's kingdom, they had something I envied and desperately needed. They were the ones who were rich.

That's when I began my journey toward *enough*.

Let Me Break This to You Gently—You're Rich!

Did you know that if you are an American or if you live what would be considered a middle-class lifestyle in Western culture, you are probably one of the richest people in the world? That's right. You may not have known it, but you're rich! Consider the following:

- If you have an annual income of $20,000 in the United States, you are in the top 11% of richest people in the world.

- If you have an annual income of $50,000, you are in the top 0.9% of richest people in the world.
- If you have an annual income of $100,000, you are in the top 0.6% of richest people in the world.[1]

I find those statistics to be pretty humbling. The truth is, I make over $100,000 a year. I own my house—a two-thousand-square-foot, four-bedroom, two-bath home in an old but very respectable area of Austin. And while I don't like to admit it, by the world's standards, I'm rich. As I've traveled to different parts of the world and as I've encountered scenes of unbelievable poverty, I've begun to realize just how wealthy—financially and materially—I really am. And if you're reading this book—if you actually had the financial ability to pay for it—then chances are you're rich too.

Thurston

I'd like to introduce you to a rich man. He's unnamed in the Bible, but I like to call him Thurston. Thurston is a good, rich-sounding kind of name, isn't it? (If your name happens to be Thurston and you find my commentary offensive, please forgive me. I think it comes from me being raised on a steady diet of *Gilligan's Island*.)

Here is Jesus' brief introduction of Thurston as recorded in Luke: "There was a rich man who was dressed in purple and fine linen and lived in luxury every day" (Luke 16:19). Jesus' original audience would recognize purple as the expensive dye used to color certain fabrics. It wasn't available to just anyone, and the fact that Jesus mentions it is probably meant to show us just how wealthy Thurston really was.

Jesus isn't making a moral commentary on Thurston's wealth at this point. He is in no way impugning Thurston for being rich. He's simply giving us a factual description of Thurston's earthly reality and setting up a juxtaposition with a beggar whom we'll look at later.

After introducing Thurston, Jesus tells us that he died and was buried. Then he tells us that Thurston went to hell (see Luke 16:22–23). That's a terrifying statement, and one we know is true because it is soberly delivered by the Son of God. Jesus doesn't tell us how he knew of Thurston's eternal condemnation, only the ugly reality of it. The point Jesus is making is that there is a connection between Thurston's wealth on earth and his unfortunate eternal reality: "Son, remember that in your lifetime you received your good things . . . but now . . . you are in agony" (Luke 16:25).

Welcome to the slippery slope of trying to be wealthy and godly at the same time. It's not impossible, as there are plenty of wealthy biblical characters who loved God. But Jesus did go out of his way to point out the challenges that people with significant financial resources face when recognizing their need for salvation.

Trouble in Paradise

Let's get down to brass tacks. I think I know how you may be feeling about now. You probably want to scream "Enough!" and you would be talking about having had enough of this book and of me making you feel guilty for enjoying what you have. After all, nowhere in the Bible does it say that we shouldn't own a swimming pool, a car that runs, or eighty-dollar jeans. It doesn't say that it's bad to have a nice home, or even two nice homes. So why should I feel bad for taking advantage of the culture I live in? Why should I feel bad for being rewarded with material and financial gain for working hard and doing a good job? What's the big deal with having *more than enough*?

Having money and material possessions isn't bad in and of itself, so why is having a surplus of them such a risky spiritual venture? Why did Jesus emphasize the dangers of living with *more than enough*? Here are just a few of the risks he might have had in mind:

- *Having more than enough can make you proud.* It's easy to start thinking too highly of yourself if you happen to have financial success. America is filled with stories of "self-made" men and women; but in reality, there is no such thing. Whatever success we have is a gift from God. To grow proud over our so-called accomplishments is to miss the point entirely.

- *Having more than enough can make you feel entitled.* Entitlement is believing that you're owed certain rights or privileges. It's the mind-set that as a person of status and means, you are due certain perks that others don't get and that you should be free from some of the mundane obligations others have to put up with. It's the business executive who feels that he shouldn't have to stand in the same line that everyone else does when boarding a plane. It's the church member who thinks he should have the pastor's ear because he gives a lot of money. Or it's the teenager who grows up thinking that having twice-a-year ski trips to Vail, her own room, and her own car are somehow things she's owed. Living with *more than enough* can make you feel like you're more important than you really are.

- *Having more than enough can create a false sense of security.* Those of us who consistently have more than we need can easily be lured into believing that we can't be touched by the cares of life. Between our savings accounts, our borrowing power, and our IRAs, we think we're pretty much set. But no such security exists. Troubles, temptation, sickness, and death will find us all, and no amount of money can stop them.

- *Having more than enough distracts you.* The problem with having money and things is that you have to manage it and them. Such "wealth management" takes time and can easily distract you from pursuing kingdom things. I've seen more than a few potentially high-impact Christ-followers rendered completely ineffective for God simply because they spend so much time managing what they have accumulated.

- *Having more than enough only makes you hungry for more.* Money and possessions don't satisfy. All they do is bait and switch. They promise happiness, comfort, and security, but in the end they only leave you longing for more. That's why very few of us are able to declare "Enough!" when it comes to material things—they never fulfill us. King Solomon was right when he declared, "Whoever loves money never has money enough; whoever loves wealth is never satisfied with his income. This too is meaningless" (Eccles. 5:10). Translation: "I've got everything, and it means nothing. Serious bummer!" That is why so many wealthy people seem to be trapped on a treadmill of more. They're always trying to run to the next level, get the next prize, close the next deal. But when they get there, they keep running. Their newfound prize doesn't satisfy like they hoped it would. So they keep running. Sadly, many of them run till they drop.

- *Having more than enough creates "powerful" people.* In God's economy, there is no such thing as a powerful person. There are no wheeler-dealers, no fat cats, no heavy hitters. But in this world, money brings power. Money shortens the distance between those who have it and those in places of authority.

Across from my family's lake house is a sheer rock wall that drops about 150 vertical feet from above. That canyon wall runs for several miles along that side of the lake, and a city ordinance prohibits houses or docks from being built there. The water isn't deep enough, the wall is too dangerous to build on, and the lake simply isn't wide enough to have docks on both sides. But right across from our house is a large boat dock. It's got a tramway that leads up to a house 150 feet above. The entire thing is illegal. It's a violation of several city codes. But there it sits anyway. How? The owner is a well-known Austin multimillionaire. He had the pull with the right city leaders to get variances and waivers on the city codes. That's power, and money buys it.

But such money-wielding influence isn't biblical. The resources God gives us are to be used for the benefit of others, not ourselves. That's what so many of the Old Testament prophets said about justice: it shouldn't be only for those who can pay for it. Rather, those with *more than enough* need to make sure that those with *less than enough* get justice as well.

- *Having more than enough can make you unappreciative.* Familiarity breeds contempt, including in the world of *more than enough*. Living with plenty can cause you to take for granted what you have. It can make you unappreciative. My neighbor has a son who joined the army at age eighteen. He just came back for a visit, eighteen months and nineteen countries later. He's seen the world. I asked him what he had learned. I never would have expected his response: *People over here don't appreciate what they have.* After seeing much of the impoverished world, his conclusion was that we don't get it. That's a pretty profound insight for a twenty-year-old.

When I think of the impact of having *more than enough* on the lives of men and women who are sincerely trying to follow God, I often think of Dorothy and her friends in the poppy fields outside of the Emerald City in *The Wizard of Oz*. While they desperately needed to get to the safety of the city gates, something in the fields was lulling them to sleep. They were overwhelmed by the fragrant aroma of the poppies that surrounded them and they drifted off to sleep, well short of their goal and the safe confines of the city. They did so at their own peril.

Many of us are being lulled to sleep by the false comfort and security of having *more than enough*. Without even knowing it, we're falling well short of the goal of trusting God instead of ourselves and our stuff. And like Dorothy and her friends, we're in more danger than we could ever realize.

If All I Need Is Daily Bread, Then Why Do I Have More?

Many people don't understand why preachers and other religious leaders make them feel guilty for enjoying what they have. In fact, they get downright tired of being judged and criticized for not selling all they have, giving it to the poor, and taking a vow of poverty.

After all, isn't God the source of everything? Doesn't every good and perfect gift come from him? Didn't John the Baptist teach that no one has anything except what has been given to them from heaven (John 3:27)? And didn't Solomon teach that if we have wealth we are meant to enjoy it (Eccles. 5:19)? If the Bible teaches that we are to be content with daily bread, then why does God apparently keep giving me more than what I need today? And if he is giving me more, am I wrong to enjoy it? Is he setting me up to fail, or am I missing something?

Those are great questions, and the answers aren't easy. So let's start with the basics and work from there.

[*Disclaimer: This is a guilt-free section. Whether you make a little or a lot, my intention is not to make you feel guilty for what you have. More importantly, it's not God's intention either. My intention is to simply get you thinking about *why* you have more than you need.]

First of all, everything we have is indeed from God. Name your blessing or gift—material, spiritual, relational. You don't have anything that God hasn't given you. The breath you just exhaled and that last blood-pumping beat of your heart are gifts from God. The eyes you're using to read this and the brain you're using to process the information are from God. The clothes you're wearing, the money in your wallet, the place where you live—they're all from God.

Second, you're not wrong to enjoy these things. Being thankful for and enjoying what God has given you is a great way to worship God and to remain humble before him. Paul wrote, "So whether you eat or drink or whatever you do, do it all for the glory of God" (1 Cor. 10:31).

Third (and here's the *but* that you knew was coming), your *more than enough* isn't just for your enjoyment. With every blessing, with every opportunity, and with every bit of favor that God gives you comes the equal responsibility to use it well. Rarely if ever does God give you blessings that he intends you to keep for yourself. He typically blesses you so you can serve and bless others. The *more than enough* he gives you is meant to be shared so that it can become *enough* for someone else. If you're living today with more than you need—not more than you'll need the next ten years, but more than you need today—then that surplus is meant to be shared. If I live with *more than enough* and somehow interpret that as God's blessing to me and me alone, then I am greatly misinterpreting why God has chosen to bless me. He isn't just being good to me; he wants to be good to someone else through me.

A More Excellent Way

> All the believers were together and had everything in common. Selling their possessions and goods, they gave to anyone as he had need. (Acts 2:44–45)

I find this summary statement of life in the Jerusalem church in the months following Pentecost to be both inspiring and humbling. The heartfelt sharing of resources by these early believers challenges me to hold very loosely what God has given me. It's one of the clearest biblical pictures of those with *more than enough* using their resources wisely.

But to many, and especially to those who read these words with any sort of experience with communism or socialism, this passage can be a bit troubling. Without knowing the backdrop, it can sound somewhat like Christian communism. It wasn't. Let me quickly walk you through what makes this Christian sharing so unique and beautiful.

In the weeks and months after the Jewish Feast of Pentecost and the outpouring of God's Spirit recorded by Luke in Acts 2:1–4, thousands of Jewish pilgrims who had traveled to Jerusalem for the celebration probably decided to extend their stays. Many of those—Luke tells us thousands of them—came to faith in Christ in the following months. It couldn't have been too long before those travelers began to see their own resources dwindle. The new Christians who lived in Jerusalem or those who had brought an abundance of provision suddenly found themselves with the opportunity to serve and share with their new Christian brothers and sisters. They took them into their homes and openly shared their goods with them.

I must point out that there was no governing agency overseeing this distribution of goods or requiring it in any way. In fact, in contrast to socialism or communism, this sharing of resources was completely:

1. Spontaneous—the believers gave as they wanted to and felt led to.
2. Voluntary—not compulsory. Not every believer participated in the sharing. Probably not every believer had the means to.

3. Sacrificial—this wasn't Beverly Hills. This was first-century AD Jerusalem, a town that was barely subsisting under the brutal hand of its Roman invaders. While there may have been some wealthy Jews in this early congregation, most would have been poor. And yet they still readily shared what they had.

4. Motivated by love—the only driving force behind the generosity was love. These new believers were extremely grateful for the chance to have their sins forgiven, to be living in the days of fulfilled prophecy as they had come to know the promised Messiah. They would have been thrilled to have God's once elusive and unpredictable Spirit now indwelling them. Their love for their new Savior and their new brothers and sisters is what drove their generosity.

As I reflect on these verses, I'm tempted to try to write off these believers' generosity as some sort of first-century spiritual phenomenon that wasn't meant to become the standard for all of us. Times change. Life is different today. Who am I to go nosing around my neighbors' or my Christian friends' lives in the hopes of finding someone I can help? It's none of my business, right? Wouldn't they be embarrassed for me to know?

And what about the poor around the world? How can they be my problem? I don't know them. Our paths never cross. If they happen to live in a country that's poor, or if they live under the rule of an oppressive government, is that my problem? If God in his infinite wisdom saw fit to have them born into poverty and me born into affluence, shouldn't that be the end of the story?

Like I said, I want to write off these verses as not really applying to me. But so far, I haven't been very successful.

Sometime Island

Just northwest of Austin is a gorgeous body of water known as Lake Travis. Lake Travis, created by the damming of the Colorado River in 1941, is 64 miles long, has a maximum width of 4.5 miles, and covers nearly 19,000 acres. It plays host to Jet Skiing, waterskiing, boating, sailing, swimming, scuba diving, and fishing, and is lined by dozens of beautiful resorts and restaurants. Austin residents know Lake Travis as one of their favorite year-round playgrounds.

But that's not why it was created. Lake Travis was designed to be a giant reservoir, a huge holding tank that allows the flow of the Colorado River to be restricted as it heads downstream to the Gulf of Mexico. East of Austin the Colorado flows through some rich farm and ranch land—land that desperately needs water. In the late 1930s, creative engineers figured out that if they could slow down the flow of the Colorado, they could build up a water supply to help out those farmers when they needed it. When the state gets dry and the farmers need the water, engineers can release some to the landowners downstream. As a result, Lake Travis is not a constant-level lake. Its level can rise or fall anywhere from ten to fifty feet over the course of a year or two. This, of course, drives homeowners around the lake crazy as they have to adjust their docks and waterfront property to the ever-changing water levels. It also means that islands will appear and disappear on Lake Travis, depending on the water level.

Sometime Island is a small section of dirt and rock that first appears whenever the lake gets to be more than ten to fifteen feet below full. It's located close to a major highway that passes by the lake, so residents and travelers alike can easily see it. Some clever person nicknamed it Sometime Island because sometimes it's there and sometimes it isn't. At the time of this writing, Lake Travis is getting low and Sometime Island has been exposed for over a year. That always leads to a healthy growth of weeds and plants on the island, which only adds to its "charm." Occasionally, a real estate For Sale sign will show up on Sometime Island. Pretty funny.

I often point to Lake Travis as a metaphor for how God uses us and our resources. There are times you're going to be very full—you'll feel well funded, well provided for, and very secure. You'll have *much more than enough*. But then needs are going to come up around you. Drought is going to come to someone's life. God is going to ask you to send what he has given you to someone else who needs it more than you do. And when you obey him, when you release your resources, your level of *more than enough* is going to drop. You won't be anywhere near empty, but you'll have less than you did. And as that pattern repeats itself in your life, your level of provision will decrease even more. Islands of scarcity might begin to pop up in your life. You might feel less secure, less protected, and less able to enjoy what you have.

When that happens, think about why God gives us *more than enough*. We, like Lake Travis, are reservoirs. We really enjoy being full, but that's not why we were created. We were made to be holding tanks for God's resources; he gives them to us to hold only until someone really needs them. And as we release what God gives us, as we begin to see our provision levels drop, God promises to always resupply us. We will never run dry.

In my lifetime I've seen Lake Travis set records on both ends of the spectrum—from flood stage to record lows with Sometime Islands popping up everywhere. And whichever end of the spectrum the lake is at, I know that it won't be too long before things change. If the lake is low, the rains will eventually come. They always do. If the lake is full, then I can expect the lake level to start dropping soon. That's what it was made for. And when it does, when Sometime Island pops up, I can rest in the fact that somewhere downstream thirsty crops and livestock are being watered, and some farmer or rancher is giving thanks to God.

Moving Toward Enough

From Jimmy: My outlook really began to change while lying in a bunk bed in Mexico. I had been listening to a former Mexican gang member talk about his salvation and the work he was now doing. Later, as I processed what God had been teaching me, it became harder and harder for me to reconcile how we lived. I could no longer justify it, and I knew we had to make a change. That started our process of moving toward living with less. . . . You have to be willing to be quiet. You have to give God his proper place. Have the courage to follow where he's leading you. On the other side of every step of obedience is more intimacy with Jesus. Pray for courage and wisdom. Trust that God is good.

For Further Reflection

1. Read Proverbs 15:16 and reflect on why the Bible claims that faith yields more joy than riches do.
2. Read Matthew 6:33 and meditate on what it means to seek first God's kingdom and God's righteousness.
3. Reflect on the image of Sometime Island. How might that be a metaphor for what God wants to do in your life? Be honest about how that makes you feel. Does it excite you, scare you, or anger you? Try to put your feelings into words.

5

Smog

smog (noun): 1. a fog made heavier and darker
by smoke and chemical fumes; 2. a photochemi-
cal haze caused by the action of solar ultraviolet
radiation on atmosphere polluted with hydro-
carbons and oxides of nitrogen especially from
automobile exhaust;[1] 3. a vision that God gave me.

Oscar's church is located in a rough-and-tumble section of
Managua, Nicaragua. Nicaragua is a country known around
the world for the terrible earthquake that rocked Managua in
1972, for the Sandinistas' subsequent rise to power, and for
the scandalous Iran-Contra affair that marked the Reagan
administration in the mid-1980s. What is often overlooked
about Nicaragua is its terrible poverty. Oscar's church is located in one of the most desperate and impoverished sec-
tions of Managua. Oscar felt led to serve the people in that

difficult part of town, and so he planted a church right in the middle of it.

Trash and filth line the streets. Groups of men—young and old—loiter on corners and pass the time by drinking and harassing the young girls and women who live in the area. It's not uncommon to find eight to twelve people—usually women and children—living in makeshift shelters no larger than the average American kitchen. They make easy prey for the men hanging around just outside. It's terrible.

And there in the middle of all the despair is Oscar's church—Rey Solomon (King Solomon). Actually, Oscar's church also houses a Christian school and center for special needs education. Oscar, his family, and staff all live among the people they serve. They share their poverty. But for nearly twenty years Oscar's ministry has brought hope to countless souls in this area.

A few years ago, I had the privilege of worshiping in Oscar's church. It was a Tuesday night and the little room was packed with well over a hundred eager worshipers. You need to see this in your mind to appreciate it—a one-room church building with a small, raised wood platform in front. There was an ancient sound system that only worked when cranked up to full volume. A battered wood floor was covered with cheap plastic chairs. The room had no air-conditioning and poor lighting.

But the church that met there was very much alive. For the better part of three hours we sang, danced, chanted, jumped, cheered, clapped, celebrated, and screamed at the top of our voices to the God who was the hope of those desperate people. Rarely have I been in such a joy-filled worship setting.

Please keep in mind that this little church was something most of us would be ashamed to enter if it was in our town. It wouldn't meet our comfort standards. We certainly wouldn't leave our kids there. And we'd never invite our friends. We demolish church buildings like Oscar's. But the people of Rey Solomon will not let themselves be defined by their material standing. Their suffering and desperation were expressed in their passionate and heartfelt encounter with the living God. It was the kind of worship encounter, I should add, that I have rarely experienced in my cozy church confines back home.

During the three-hour worship and preaching event, I had a vision. That I had any type of spiritual encounter at all is nothing less than a miracle. The church service was held entirely in Spanish, which means I was able to pick up about one out of every ten thousand words. Beyond that, there was some serious speaking in tongues going on around me. I'm not one who has any specific type of tongue-speaking or interpreting ability, but I recognize that many of my Christian brothers and sisters do. I've prayed in enough denominationally mixed Christian settings to feel comfortable when those around me are praying in tongues. Actually, I think it's kind of cool. My point is that given the language barriers, I wasn't really set up to have a profound spiritual experience. But I had one nonetheless. During the worship, I saw a vision, a picture in my mind. I'll never get over it.

I saw my homeland from a great distance, as if I were actually looking at it from Nicaragua. I saw our cities, our beautiful landscapes, our homes, and our churches. Covering the whole scene, shrouding everything in our great nation, was a thick blanket of smog. It clung to our cities, our families, and our churches like the death angel in Exodus. There was no place that wasn't being poisoned by it. It was a distressing sight, almost as if this dense cloud of smog was choking the very life out of my country.

What was this smog? What did I see that was choking the life out of our great land? Materialism. The shroud that was killing the life in our families, cities, and churches was in fact the financial and material prosperity that so many of us enjoy. We're dying from it, drowning in it, and we don't even see it.

Of course, it took a trip to Managua and a Spirit-filled worship event with a group of terribly suffering people for me to see just how impotent and materially bound my own life and ministry had become. We put way too much emphasis on our buildings and budgets and not nearly enough on the power of God's Holy Spirit. We've substituted monetary wealth and society's definition of success for God's riches and God's favor. We've chosen convenience over anointing, comfort over conviction. We think we're rich, but in reality we are the ones who are poor.

It was a shattering moment for me. I looked around that room of relatively uneducated and severely impoverished believers—people I had felt sorry for when I first entered the room—and I realized that they were the ones who got it. Through their terrible circumstances and suffering they had figured out what really matters. And I—well-clothed, well-educated, and well-paid—realized that I was the one in the room who was missing something.

I remember sitting down on my plastic folding chair and repenting right then and there before God. I confessed my addiction to stuff and my lack of pursuit of God's true presence and power in my life. I was living in a smog-filled world and I hadn't even noticed. The implications of that vision for my life and ministry have been far-reaching. I'm still a long way from knowing just how far-reaching it will be, but this I do know—those of us in Western culture are being choked out by the stuff we've surrounded ourselves with. Our *more than enough* status in life may actually be the one thing that's hindering God's work in us the most.

I'm Fine!

How do you typically respond when someone asks you how you're doing? Unless it's a close friend or a paid professional counselor, most of us have a canned response: "I'm great," "Hanging in there," or one of my personal favorites, "Peachy!" We answer quickly because we know that the person asking is typically just being polite, doesn't have time for a long answer, and may not really even care how we are. So we respond equally politely and move on.

One of my closest friends is a Christian counselor who likes to make fun of one particular trite response to the "How are you?" question. When people respond with "Fine," he tells them what he believes the letters in FINE stand for: frenzied, insecure, neurotic, and emotional. That adds a whole new meaning to the word *fine*, doesn't it? And in reality, my friend's meaning of *fine* may actually be closer to the truth. While many of us look put together and successful on the outside, on the inside we're a mess.

Jesus once addressed a group of Christians at the ancient church of Laodicea. Laodicea was located in Asia Minor and was known for its wealthy citizens, its commerce, and its banking industry. When the city was almost completely destroyed by a series of earthquakes in AD 60–61, the citizens were able to quickly rebuild at their own expense, rejecting any offers of imperial aid. The Laodiceans were a hearty, pull-yourself-up-by-your-bootstraps, independent folk. Were you to ask them how they were doing, they'd probably respond, "Fine, just fine"—and mean it. And for that, Jesus took them to task.

Here's part of Jesus' message to them:

> To the angel of the church in Laodicea write: These are the words of the Amen, the faithful and true witness, the ruler of God's creation. I know your deeds, that you are neither cold nor hot. I wish you were either one or the other! So, because you are lukewarm—neither hot nor cold—I am about to spit you out of my mouth. You say, "I am rich; I have acquired wealth and do not need a thing." But you do not realize that you are wretched, pitiful, poor, blind and naked. I counsel you to buy from me gold refined in the fire, so you can become rich; and white clothes to wear, so you can cover your shameful nakedness; and salve to put on your eyes, so you can see. (Rev. 3:14–18)

In other words, Jesus was basically saying, "You keep saying you're fine, and I agree! You're frenzied, insecure, neurotic, and emotional. You're not doing as well as you think you are. In fact, you're sick, very sick, and you need my help immediately."

When I think of my smog vision, that's what I think of. I see many of us rolling along as if everything is just rosy, and all the while Jesus is shaking his head saying, "You guys just don't get it." His counsel to the Laodicean believers applies to us as well: *Come to me; let me give you life; let me cover you with my protection; let me be your hope, otherwise you're bankrupt.*

In contrast, consider Paul's description of the believers in Macedonia: "And now, brothers, we want you to know about the grace that God has given the Macedonian churches. Out of the most severe trial, their overflowing joy and their extreme poverty welled up in rich generosity" (2 Cor. 8:1–2). Did you catch those interesting juxtapositions? "Severe trial" yielded "overflowing joy," and "extreme poverty" produced "rich generosity." What a difference from the believers in Laodicea! Even though the Macedonians' financial portfolio was significantly less than stellar, their joy and generosity were off the charts. So what's the difference? Why did the Laodiceans, who appeared to have so much, lack what the Macedonians, who appeared to have so little, had. Once again we find the Bible teaching that joy and contentment don't come with wealth; rather, they typically increase when we live with less.

Rise Up and Walk

I've read multiple accounts of a conversation that took place in the thirteenth century between Thomas Aquinas and Pope Innocent IV. The story goes that Thomas called on the pope one day while he was overseeing the counting of a large sum of money for the church. The pope greeted Thomas and said with a smile, "See, Thomas, the church can no longer say, 'Silver and gold have we none.'"

The pope was referencing the magnificent story in Acts 3 where Peter and John met a lame beggar in the temple courts in Jerusalem. The beggar asked the two disciples for a gift. Peter, under the leadership of the Holy Spirit, responded, "Silver or gold I do not have, but what I have I give you. In the name of Jesus Christ of Nazareth, walk" (3:6). The subsequent scene—the formerly lame man dancing and jumping around the temple—caused quite a stir and landed Peter and John in jail (see Acts 3–4).

Thomas considered the pope's comment and then replied, "That's true, Holy Father. But we can no longer say 'Rise up and walk.'"

Basically, that was the point of my vision. We live comfortable lives and live in nice homes; we have beautiful church buildings and we dress up in fine clothes for worship—but we're spiritually anemic. The primary culprit behind our chronic weakness is our addiction to material things.

The Difference between a Rich Man and a Camel

It's one of the most familiar word pictures in Jesus' teaching, and probably one of the most misquoted as well. I'm talking about the statement Jesus made to his disciples after his conversation with a man who has come to be known as the Rich Young Ruler (see Luke 18:18–25). After Jesus challenged the man to let go of his wealth, give it to the poor, and simply follow him, the man "became very sad, because he was a man of great wealth" (Luke 18:23). Upon seeing the rich man's response, Jesus offered the following insight: "How hard it is for the rich to enter the kingdom of God! Indeed, it is easier for a camel to go through the eye of a needle than for a rich man to enter the kingdom of God" (vv. 24–25).

The part of Jesus' story that most folks remember is the camel and the eye of the needle. That fascinates people. The idea of a camel literally trying to go through the eye of a needle is ridiculous. Jesus was obviously using hyperbole to make a point. But unfortunately, many people still don't hear Jesus' message. Jesus never said that it's impossible for those with *more than enough* to get to heaven, but he did say it can be very difficult.

What people often don't know is that scholars believe there was a narrow gate in the Jerusalem wall called the Needle. It was designed for pedestrian access only. A merchant or traveler who was bringing goods into the city via camel would most likely not be able to use this entrance, as it would be next to impossible for the fully burdened beast to fit through the opening. Jesus may have been referencing this gate when he made the statement. Either way, Jesus' point was that those who are burdened with wealth often find their financial and material loads prohibitive to their spiritual progress. He was saying that having *more than enough* tends to hinder, not help, one's ability to know and love God.

The Death Zone

It's called the Death Zone. It is the harshest, most unfriendly environment into which any human can venture. The Death Zone is the term given by mountaineers to those peaks where elevations reach above 26,000 feet (8,000 meters). Let me put that into perspective. Denver, Colorado, the Mile High City, rests at 5,280 feet (exactly one mile) above sea level. Leadville, Colorado, at 10,081 feet, is the highest incorporated city in the United States and is nearly a mile higher than Denver. If you don't live in the mountains and then visit a town with a high elevation, you immediately feel the difference. The air is thinner, and the higher you go the thinner it gets. Your body has less oxygen to work with, and that can make even the most basic activities quite taxing.

The tallest mountains in the world are four miles higher than Denver. Men and women who climb to those altitudes put an incredible strain on their bodies. They simply don't get enough oxygen to survive, which is why most carry small oxygen tanks when they make their summit pushes. At 26,000 feet above sea level, it's just a matter of time before your body shuts down. Only a handful of people in the world can climb to those altitudes without supplemental oxygen and live. If you and I were instantly transported Star Trek–style to the summit of one of those mountains, we'd be dead in minutes. Our bodies weren't designed to live there.

I think that's what Jesus was saying when he talked about the perils of mixing wealth and spiritual pursuits. Instead of aiding spirituality, money and possessions inhibit it. It's as if people with *more than enough* have moved into a zone where humans weren't designed to live. Rather than making our lives better, material glut chokes the life out of us. And those traits in humans that God wants to develop—faith, simplicity, generosity, dependence—are frequently muted by the conditions in the Material Death Zone. We quickly succumb to stress, busyness, greed, covetousness, stinginess, the allure of power, the sense of entitlement, a false sense of security, and independence from God. Only a handful of people throughout history have proven to have what it takes to manage wealth and to thrive spiritually at the same time. In the process of trying to manage having *more than enough*, most people lose what really matters.

Are You Choking in the Smog?

What do you think? Is the smog getting the best of you? Are you succumbing to the poisonous gases of materialism? Are you slowly losing your spiritual vitality in the dangerously thin air of the Death Zone?

The Bible offers a surprisingly simple solution to the problem of smog that I saw in my vision. In a word, it's generosity. Men and women who are willing to generously share what God has given them will stay free from the pull of more that is such a normal part of living in a relatively rich culture. If materialism is the smog that is choking out our spiritual life, then generosity is the wind that will blow the smog away.

To stay with the metaphor a bit longer, to effectively deal with the smog issue in our country, those of us who have *more than enough* need to move toward the Bible's definition of *enough*. Stated more bluntly, we have to jettison some of our material cargo.

In his book *No Shortcuts to the Top*, mountaineer Ed Viesturs (who is, by the way, one of the few men in the world who has climbed to 26,000 feet or higher without supplemental oxygen and lived to tell about it) talks about a prank the mountain guides used to play on each other when he was guiding on Mt. Rainier. They would secretly drop a small rock into the pack of one of their fellow guides, and they would do it repeatedly over the course of several days. At first, the weight difference was negligible. But when the rock count reached about twenty, those added pounds would begin to make a huge difference in the person's performance at high altitudes. Some guides would figure out that they'd been "rocked." Others would struggle up the hill until one of their more compassionate teammates would let them in on the joke.

Material possessions are like that. The more you have, the more cumbersome and difficult to manage they become. At first you may not notice the difference. But the more you try to pursue God and carry your riches along with you, the more burdensome your stuff will become.

Maybe that's why Jesus gave such a simple definition of *enough*. Maybe that's why the Bible teaches that the best way to deal with stuff is to give it away.

King Solomon reflected on the importance of releasing one's wealth when he wrote, "A generous man will prosper; he who refreshes others will himself be refreshed" (Prov. 11:25). It's nearly impossible to argue with the simplicity and clarity of those words: If you use what you have to refresh others, then you yourself will be refreshed. But the opposite is true as well. If you hoard what you have, it will wear you down.

Do you want to get rid of your smog? Pray for the fresh winds of generosity to blow through your life. Your generous spirit will not only benefit others, it will also strengthen your own spiritual condition.

Moving Toward Enough

From Keith and Leanna: First, buy a car that isn't a status symbol. Doing so will tell you a lot about yourself. A car is the only possession that you take everywhere you go. I've been guilty of thinking I was smarter, better looking, and cooler when I rolled up—even to a stoplight—in a luxury SUV. I have finally recovered from the cool car syndrome! I love having no car payment and not getting my self-worth from a machine.

For Further Reflection

1. Reread Revelation 3:14–18, and then rewrite it as you think Jesus might speak it to you and your community today.

2. Reread Luke 18:24–25 and list as many reasons as you can for why it's so hard for rich people to get to heaven.
3. Pray about ways you can remove the smog of materialism from your life. Then list three or four of your best ideas and start applying them.

6

Thorns

thorn (noun): a woody plant bearing sharp imped-
ing processes (as prickles or spines); or, something
that causes distress or irritation.[1]

The Thorny Trifecta

Jesus wasn't a fan of riches. I mean, he wasn't anti-wealth, but
he just didn't have a lot of good things to say about money
and possessions, especially when set in a context of *more than
enough*. At least that's the impression I get when I read his
teachings. In one well-known parable, Jesus compared riches
to the thorns that choke out the desirable plants in a garden.

The parable of the sower (also known as the parable of the
seed) is recorded in the first three Gospels (see Matt. 13:1–23;
Mark 4:1–20; and Luke 8:1–15). I believe the prominence
the biblical writers give it underscores the significance of
Jesus' teaching to his original hearers. It's quite a profound

parable, with many implications for the lives of believers and unbelievers alike.

In the parable, Jesus compared the gospel message to a seed that a farmer would sow. He then illustrated the different responses people have to the gospel by describing different types of soil and how each responds to sown seed. The third type of soil Jesus described was thorny: "Other seed fell among thorns, which grew up and choked the plants, so that they did not bear grain" (Mark 4:7). A little later, Jesus offered his explanation about this third soil type: "Still others, like seed sown among thorns, hear the word; but the worries of this life, the deceitfulness of wealth and the desires for other things come in and choke the word, making it unfruitful" (Mark 4:18–19). I've always found this teaching of Jesus to be both intriguing and more than a little troubling. As a guy who has always had *more than enough*, I feel the need to pay close attention to what Jesus said here.

Jesus suggested that this type of soil was made ineffective by three different types of thorns that choked out the life of the gospel. What were they?

- *The worries of this life.* Literally, "the worries of this age." Regardless of what period of history you live in, there will always be temptations and distractions that keep you from focusing on your future life in heaven. While our hearts are supposed to be set on things eternal, we often fall prey to the pull of the temporal. Thus the stuff of here and now, which is meaningless in light of eternity, steals our attention from those things that really matter.
- *The deceitfulness of wealth.* It's hard to find any gentle explanation of this one. Wealth is false advertising. It

promises things it can never deliver. Think about it: Does that new car really make you sexier, cooler, or more attractive? Does that larger home really give you anything more than higher property taxes? And, much more seriously, how many men and women have sacrificed their eternal souls in the pursuit of more that wealth ultimately never delivers? Jesus called it the deceitfulness of wealth for a reason. It's a lie.

- *The desires for other things.* In case anything was left uncovered by his first two categories, Jesus added this third to sum it all up. The *lust for other things* spotlights those desires for things not specifically included in the groups of worry and wealth—popularity, pleasure, power, and other "other things." I'm sure you could list your own. While many of these other things aren't necessarily bad in themselves, when given priority over following the gospel, they become deadly.

Follow the Money

Recently, our church helped fund a survey of the spiritual climate of our city. It was one of the most thorough studies of a city's spiritual landscape ever done in the United States. One of the things we were able to discern from the survey is how there are physical pockets of both faith and disbelief in our city. You can literally mark them on a map. Tragically, and quite disheartening to me personally, was the revelation that the area of town I grew up in, an area characterized by both great wealth and high educational levels, had the highest degree of spiritual skepticism and religious inactivity in our city. Those people in my hometown who seemingly have been given the most believe the least. What a sad reality. And what a confirmation of Jesus' teachings about wealth, thorns, and receptiveness to his message.

Solomon

He had everything. I mean everything.

Solomon, son of King David and heir to the throne of Israel, led his nation to its highest levels of military, economic, political, and geographic dominance. Solomon was arguably one of the greatest leaders in world history. He was also one of the wealthiest. Solomon's great wisdom was famous throughout the known world, and it led many other world leaders to heap gifts and riches on him, both as expressions of honor and as not-so-subtle attempts to win his favor.

Solomon lived on a level of pleasure and comfort that few in history have ever known. Here's his own description of his pleasures:

> I undertook great projects: I built houses for myself and planted vineyards. I made gardens and parks and planted all kinds of fruit trees in them. I made reservoirs to water groves of flourishing trees. I bought male and female slaves and had other slaves who were born in my house. I also owned more herds and flocks than anyone in Jerusalem before me. I amassed silver and gold for myself, and the treasure of kings and provinces. I acquired male and female singers, and a harem as well—the delights of the heart of man. I became greater by far than anyone in Jerusalem before me. In all this my wisdom stayed with me. I denied myself nothing my eyes desired; I refused my heart no pleasure. (Eccles. 2:4–10)

And God was behind all of it. He promised Solomon that if he remained faithful to him and stayed humble, he would give him both wisdom and wealth. He would make Solomon an example of his favor for all to see. And God did that faithfully for many years.

Could you handle that? Could you handle wealth and wisdom in exchange for loyalty to God? Sounds simple, right? But Solomon couldn't. Solomon was the wisest man on earth, but he couldn't resist the allure of more. He had more wealth, power, and prestige than any other human at his time, but he still wasn't content. He started looking at what God hadn't given him, not what God had given him. His downfall? Women.

> King Solomon, however, loved many foreign women besides Pharaoh's daughter—Moabites, Ammonites, Edomites, Sidonians and Hittites. They were from nations about which the LORD had told the Israelites, "You must not intermarry with them, because they will surely turn your hearts after their gods." Nevertheless, Solomon held fast to them in love. (1 Kings 11:1–2)

In the name of expanding his kingdom through politically arranged marriages and to satisfy his own out-of-control sexual urges, Solomon violated a basic law of God. Here's the tragic summary of Solomon's poor choices:

> As Solomon grew old, his wives turned his heart after other gods, and his heart was not fully devoted to the LORD his God, as the heart of David his father had been. He followed Ashtoreth the goddess of the Sidonians, and Molech the detestable god of the Ammonites. So Solomon did evil in the eyes of the LORD; he did not follow the LORD completely, as David his father had done. (1 Kings 11:4–6)

Once again, the allure of more won out. Solomon reached for the same tree as Adam and Eve. And in his effort to get what he didn't have, to get for himself what God hadn't chosen to give him, Solomon lost everything. Sound familiar?

Jubilee

God commanded his people to rest every seventh day as an act of worship and obedience to him. But did you know that God also commanded his people to rest their land every seven years?

> The LORD said to Moses on Mount Sinai, "Speak to the Israelites and say to them: 'When you enter the land I am going to give you, the land itself must observe a sabbath to the LORD. For six years sow your fields, and for six years prune your vineyards and gather their crops. But in the seventh year the land is to have a sabbath of rest, a sabbath to the LORD. Do not sow your fields or prune your vineyards. Do not reap what grows of itself or harvest the grapes of your untended vines. The land is to have a year of rest.'" (Lev. 25:1–5)

For a nation of farmers and ranchers, this must have been one seriously scary command. This Sabbath year prohibited the Israelites from working their land or cultivating it in any way. God promised to give them enough produce in the sixth year harvest to last all the way through the Sabbath year. In the same way that God provided twice the manna on the sixth day of the week so his people wouldn't have to gather on the Sabbath (during their forty years of wilderness wandering), he promised to do the same in the year before the Sabbath year.

But God added yet another dimension to his command:

92

Count off seven sabbaths of years—seven times seven years—
so that the seven sabbaths of years amount to a period of
forty-nine years. Then have the trumpet sounded everywhere
on the tenth day of the seventh month; on the Day of Atone-
ment sound the trumpet throughout your land. Consecrate
the fiftieth year and proclaim liberty throughout the land to
all its inhabitants. It shall be a jubilee for you; each one of you
is to return to his family property and each to his own clan.
The fiftieth year shall be a jubilee for you; do not sow and do
not reap what grows of itself or harvest the untended vines.
For it is a jubilee and is to be holy for you; eat only what is
taken directly from the fields. (Lev. 25:8–12)

Now that's a radical economic strategy. The Jubilee year (year
fifty after seven Sabbath years) called for the forgiving of
all debts, the returning to the original owners any land that
had been sold in the previous forty-nine years, the freeing of
anyone (and his or her family) sold into slavery in the last
forty-nine years, and again giving the land the year off from
being cultivated. That meant that in the Jubilee year landowners couldn't work their land for two consecutive years.
Again, God's promise was to give enough provision in the
forty-eighth year to last until the harvest in the fifty-first year.

If you're a business owner, you're probably thinking, "If
I did that in my business, I'd never survive." And that was
exactly God's point. He designed the Sabbath and Jubilee
years to teach his people some critical lessons. In other words,
he wanted to address some of the issues that were developing
in his people's lives. Here are just a few of them:

- *Independence.* We are too quick to forget that we are
  ultimately dependent on God, not on our productivity.

It would have been easy for the Israelite farmers to start looking to their land, not their God, as their hope. In today's world of self-made men and women, of successful businesses that were started in garages, apartments, and storage sheds, this is a good lesson for us to learn as well.

- *Misplaced priorities.* Relationships are more important than resources; people should take priority over prosperity. By asking his people to forgive all debts and to release all slaves, God was making a strong statement about what was most important in life. He simply didn't want relationships severed over financial matters or material things. The Jubilee year reestablished the priority of people and relationships over commerce and profitability. And that is another lesson we definitely need to learn today. How many siblings have you seen become bitter enemies over the settling of an estate? How many marriages have failed as one or both spouses have spent more time pursuing material things rather than cultivating their relationship?

- *Improper perspective.* I'm way too quick to see myself as owning what I have: my house, my car, my laptop. But in reality, I don't own anything. That's part of why God created the Jubilee year—to remind us that we're tenants on his land: "The land must not be sold permanently, because the land is mine and you are but aliens and my tenants. Throughout the country that you hold as a possession, you must provide for the redemption of the land" (Lev. 25:23–24). God never wanted his people to forget where they'd come from. They had been slaves in Egypt; soon they would be living freely in the Promised

Land. But the land wasn't theirs; it was his. We're no different. We can't really claim to own anything. Everything we have is a gift from God—everything. We are simply stewards and tenants.

Cory

Cory was a successful guy. He'd done well in business, was well educated, handsome, athletic, had a beautiful wife and three great kids, and was well liked among his peers. Cory was also a Christian. He loved God and did his best to live a Christ-honoring life. Cory and his family were regulars in church; he and a buddy even served together in the children's ministry.

In many ways, Cory was a stereotypical *more than enough* Christian. If you go to school and work hard at what you do, you're bound to get ahead in this life. Our culture is wired to reward guys like Cory. But what our culture does not do is show you how to manage having *more than enough*. There's never a finish line. Successful guys like Cory, if they follow the path of the typical Christian, will never take their foot off the gas pedal. They usually don't rethink their priorities or wonder why they have more than they need. Not without an ambush.

And that's why I invited Cory to Nicaragua with me. I have found that a trip to the land of *less than enough* is a great shot of reality for guys with *more than enough*. So Cory and several other guys joined me for a few days in Managua.

It's common for us while in Managua to do food distributions. We go to a local grocer, buy as much beans, rice, flour, soap, and detergent as we can, divide them up, and then go to extremely poor areas and hand out the food to desperate families. The small bags we hand out can last a family of five to seven people for up to two weeks. In some cases, the food we give is literally a lifesaver to the people we serve.

Food distributions are both the high points and the low points of our trips. The people are so gracious and kind, and we always leave feeling so blessed to have met them. But the poverty is devastating. It's nearly impossible to describe the levels of human suffering we see.

On the day that Cory's group did the distribution, we went to an area I hadn't been to before. It was one of the worst I'd seen. People lived in makeshift huts patched together with cardboard, scraps of sheet metal, discarded tires, and barbed wire. All of the huts were small; some had two or three families living in them. Children ran about on the muddy roads in their dirty underwear as they didn't own any clothes or shoes. Chickens, along with stray and starving dogs, wandered freely about, and raw sewage lay in the roads. And this "neighborhood" went on in all four directions as far as we could see.

In one of the homes we visited, I asked Cory to make the presentation to the family. Through a translator we typically tell the family that we are there in the name of Jesus and that we hope our food will encourage them and remind them of his love for them. We ask them how we can pray for them and then we circle up, join hands, and pray that God would meet their needs. Every home visit I've done has been different and every one equally powerful. This visit was no exception.

Nicaraguans have a delightful habit of praying out loud all at the same time. They don't go one at a time like we do; they just all jump in together, even if someone is leading the group. Sort of like a prayer free-for-all. It's a heavenly sound, especially when the group includes children. It's amazing to hear their young voices all praying at the same time.

As we started praying, I listened to the group. It was beautiful. Then I heard this wailing; it was almost a high-pitched moan. It was a devastating, terrible cry. Someone was in pain; someone was really grieving in prayer. I thought it was the grandmother, the gentlewoman and matriarch of the home to whom we had given the food. I just assumed that the joy over God's provision mixed with the stress of her impoverished existence had gotten the best of her. It wouldn't be the first time I'd seen that. I opened my eyes to confirm my theory and see if I could comfort the woman, but she wasn't the one who was crying.

It was Cory. My sophisticated, successful, athletic, handsome friend was gazing up in the air, crying his eyes out. He was broken, totally broken. I remained silent until the prayer was over. After we said our good-byes and headed toward the next home, I caught up with Cory. He was still teary. Our conversation went something like this:

ME: Dude, you OK?

CORY: Yes.

ME: What was that about?

CORY: I've never felt like that. I mean, when we were praying, my whole life flashed before my eyes.

ME: I don't understand.

CORY: It was like God showed me in that one moment how much my life has revolved around me. Everything I've done, it's been about me. I've lived forty-five years with me at the center of my world. And he busted me; I mean he *really* busted me. I think he's telling me it's time for me to stop living for myself and to stop pursuing things that don't matter.

With Cory's permission, I've shared this story in our church and have included it here. And yet whenever I tell the story, Cory always corrects me on one point. He says he wasn't crying; that it must have been someone else. Yeah, right.

I caught up with Cory recently and asked him how that day in Nicaragua four years ago had changed him. I wanted to know how he was living differently. In short, he's never been the same. He returns to Nicaragua every year and has had a clear change of focus in what he lives for. Here's some of what he told me.

First, he said that he is much more grateful for what he has. His exposure to poverty has totally changed how he views his own life. As a result, his personal gratitude levels have soared. Second, Cory has started helping others in his own spheres of influence. Cory realized that you don't have to travel to a third world country to find people in need. It may just be that he's more aware of needs around him, but since that day in Nicaragua Cory has been able to help several people with their own financial or material needs. Third, Cory is rethinking how he uses his own resources. He and his family have a nice home—what many would call a dream home. But they know it's not really theirs. Cory and his wife are praying about how they can use their resources for kingdom purposes. Finally, and this is a curious one, Cory's business has grown. Since he came back from Nicaragua and started giving more and helping others, Cory has made more money. His platform has expanded. It's like God is saying, "Since you've started being faithful in little things, I'll give you the chance to use even more."

I've heard similar things from others like Cory who have started moving toward *enough*. Once they see the more excellent way of living with less, they never look back.

Moving Toward Enough

From D'Ann: We just had our son's wedding. The bride and groom were very creative in their approach. They held their wedding in the community dining hall of a state park. They are avid hikers and this had been the location of their first date. We invited mostly family and close friends, and everything was "do it yourself." The menu was potluck, and one of the bridesmaids made the wedding cake. My son has never liked the wedding "trap" that people fall into. And the bride did not want to ask her parents to spend a ton of money on the wedding. We realized that the wedding is all about the people, and not the lavish dinner, booze, and decorations. We had so much fun and would not change a thing. Talk about enough? It was more than enough.

For Further Reflection

1. Read 1 Timothy 6:9–10 and list some of the temptations that wealth can bring into your life.
2. Of the three issues God addressed by requiring the Jubilee year—independence, misplaced priorities, or improper perspective—which one are you most likely to struggle with? Why?
3. Why do you think caring for those with *less than enough* has such a profound effect on those with *more than enough*?

7

Barns

more (adj.): greater (something *more* than expected); additional, further (*more* guests arrived).[1]

barn (noun): a usually large building for the storage of farm products or feed and usually for the housing of farm animals or farm equipment. Or, an unusually large and usually bare building.[2]

Decision Time

Today we have banks, safety deposit boxes, and the stock market. We have many choices when it comes to storing and/ or investing what we've earned. But in Jesus' day, they had barns. As his culture was made up primarily of farmers and ranchers, the barn would have been a prominent fixture in the landscape. So when Jesus wanted to talk about the implications of living with *more than enough*, he talked about barns:

The ground of a certain rich man produced a good crop. He thought to himself, "What shall I do? I have no place to store my crops." Then he said, "This is what I'll do. I will tear down my barns and build bigger ones, and there I will store all my grain and my goods. And I'll say to myself, 'You have plenty of good things laid up for many years. Take life easy; eat, drink and be merry.'" (Luke 12:16–19)

On the surface, this sounds like every entrepreneur's dream. In this case the guy is a farmer. His land totally goes wild and yields a bigger harvest than he ever imagined. In order to manage his new harvest, he tears down his barns and builds bigger ones. So far this sounds like a pretty good business plan, right? He's got it made. He's got enough wealth to last him for years.

There's only one problem. He had less than eight hours to live: "But God said to him, 'You fool! This very night your life will be demanded from you. Then who will get what you have prepared for yourself?'" (Luke 12:20). Okay, I'm not the sharpest tool in the shed, but I'm pretty sure that when God begins a sentence "You fool!" it can't be good news. This poor guy had missed it big-time. Not only had he wasted his money building barns to hold crops that he would never be able to take to market, but he also had presumed upon God by assuming he had years to live. From God's standpoint both errors represent serious lapses in judgment.

But perhaps the farmer's biggest mistake came at the moment that I call *Decision Time*. It came when the farmer realized that his current barns could no longer hold his crops. Jesus shared the man's rather short and one-sided thought process with us. Basically, he gave no thought to any option other than expanding what he had. That's the critical moment; that's Decision Time.

What do you do when your crops yield significant fruit? What do you do when you have a major financial gain? That's your critical moment; that's your Decision Time.

Almost without exception, people build bigger barns. It's just our natural, default instinct. If we live in a certain size house—a house that is completely adequate for our family's needs—and then we come into more money, we consider either adding on or moving to a larger house. The push is always for more, larger, nicer, bigger barns.

As a pastor, I know that the same is true for churches, and the "bigger barn" thinking is partly behind the smog that I saw in my vision in Nicaragua. Churches will rent a facility or buy a piece of land and build a small building. Then they'll start having services. God blesses their efforts and they grow. So they add a second service and they continue to grow. Pretty soon, they have so much harvest their barn is no longer adequate to hold it all. So what do they do? They build bigger barns. They tear down what they have and start over, or they sell their barns and land and buy more land and build a bigger barn.

In both cases—the individual and the church—the emphasis becomes having more, being larger, expanding assets, and increasing wealth. There's only one little problem with this strategy: nowhere in the Bible is a Christian or a church commanded to pursue more material gain. Not once. We've chosen a personal way of life and a church growth strategy that, simply stated, goes against everything the Bible teaches about stewardship, personal gain, and how we disciple people. This errant strategy is producing smog, and the smog is killing us.

So I have a simple suggestion: don't build a bigger barn. When your land yields so much produce that you're having trouble managing it, just give it away. Instead of investing in a larger house or vacation home or a backyard pool, invest it elsewhere. Declare your current barn to be large enough, then determine to give away whatever you receive that won't fit in the barn.

On the Road Again

Tim and Margaret had it all. They were raising two beautiful kids. They lived in their hometown in Ohio, and thus they were close to extended family and many lifelong friends. They were actively serving in a church they loved, and they led a thriving small group. Tim had a good, secure job that afforded him and his family a comfortable lifestyle. Their barn was full.

And then someone offered Tim a bigger barn. It came in the form of a job offer. Guys like Tim don't go unnoticed. His company's competitors saw his abilities and waved a bunch of money in front of him, more money than he ever dreamed of making. They offered to relocate Tim and his family to a new part of the country where they could have an even better lifestyle and live their dream.

What would you do? Many of us might say Tim had a moral obligation to take the money. Who wouldn't? Think of the opportunities that kind of money would give his family. Think of the security they could live with, knowing that they would always have what they needed. They could pay for college, live comfortably, and retire well. And Tim could know that he was doing something he loved, something he was good at, and that he was getting paid a boatload of money to do it. Sounds pretty good, doesn't it?

Tim and Margaret took the job. They packed up their stuff, said good-bye to their friends, family, and church, hopped on a plane with the kids, and started their new lives in Austin, Texas. That's a long way from Ohio. A few weeks later, they started attending Austin Christian Fellowship. That's when I first met them. And from the moment we first met, I could tell that they were doubting their decision. Yes, they had the more, but was it the right more? They had a much bigger barn, but was it worth it?

Rich Toward God

We probably all have a basic understanding of what it means to be wealthy. But you and I both know that there are plenty of truly rich people who live way beyond the level that we do. There's nothing wrong with that. Having *more than enough*, regardless of how much *more than enough* you have, isn't really the problem. The problem comes when we are well-off in the arena of earthly wealth but poor when it comes to what really matters. Let's revisit the farmer with the barns one more time:

> The ground of a certain rich man produced a good crop. He thought to himself, "What shall I do? I have no place to store my crops." Then he said, "This is what I'll do. I will tear down my barns and build bigger ones, and there I will store all my grain and my goods. And I'll say to myself, 'You have plenty of good things laid up for many years. Take life easy; eat, drink and be merry.'" But God said to him, "You fool! This very night your life will be demanded from you. Then

who will get what you have prepared for yourself?" This is how it will be with anyone who stores up things for himself but is not rich toward God. (Luke 12:16–21)

It's that last phrase, *rich toward God*, that grabs my attention. Jesus was not only juxtaposing having the world's wealth with having God's wealth, but he seems to be saying that it is possible to have the former without possessing the latter. And that, dear friend, can't be good.

So what does it mean to be rich toward God? The Bible offers dozens of examples of heavenly or divine wealth, but let's just focus on a few. Here are some of the more obvious examples of what it means to be rich toward God.

Being rich toward God means having a relationship with him. When you become a Christian, you immediately become part of God's family. That means that all the riches of heaven are yours. The Bible talks repeatedly about the inheritance that God's children have. As one of his kids, your eternal future is secure. You have wealth stored up that you can't even begin to measure or understand here on earth. You truly are rich.

Imagine that you made some poor business and personal decisions and accumulated more than one million dollars of debt. That would be an overwhelming amount of debt to surmount, especially when you add in interest. Then imagine that a successful businessperson decided to help you out by paying off your debt, no strings attached. One day you're a million dollars in debt, the next you're totally debt free. How would you feel? Well, besides being extremely relieved, I imagine that you might also feel rich. Because of the benevolence of another person, you just saved over a million bucks!

That's what it means to be rich toward God. We were in debt to him. The cost of our sin was something we could never pay off. We could work for all eternity and never get out of debt to God. But in the moment that you yield your life to Jesus, in the instant that you cross the line from wanderer to worshiper, all your spiritual debts are forgiven. And not only that, but you also gain all the inheritance of a child of God. It's a spiritual rags-to-riches story, and there's no way for these riches to ever be lost.

The farmer in Jesus' story missed the point. You see, it doesn't matter how rich you are on earth; if you don't have a relationship with God, you're poor.

Being rich toward God means that you're eternally, not temporally, focused. After Jesus offered this parable, he chimed in on the not-so-sacred-art of worrying:

> Therefore I tell you, do not worry about your life, what you will eat; or about your body, what you will wear. Life is more than food, and the body more than clothes. Consider the ravens: They do not sow or reap, they have no storeroom or barn; yet God feeds them. And how much more valuable you are than birds! Who of you by worrying can add a single hour to his life? Since you cannot do this very little thing, why do you worry about the rest?
>
> Consider how the lilies grow. They do not labor or spin. Yet I tell you, not even Solomon in all his splendor was dressed like one of these. If that is how God clothes the grass of the field, which is here today, and tomorrow is thrown into the fire, how much more will he clothe you, O you of little faith! And do not set your heart on what you will eat or drink; do not worry about it. For the pagan world runs after all such things, and your Father knows that you need them. But seek

his kingdom, and these things will be given to you as well. (Luke 12:22–31)

Folks who are always fretting about stuff down here can never be rich toward God. All that worrying and stressing never does any good; besides, God has already gladly given us all the wealth and authority of his kingdom. What are we worried about? People who are rich toward God don't get too wrapped up in the details of the here and now. They're looking ahead, up over the horizon, to the better life that awaits them.

People who are rich toward God don't covet, but instead are content. Remember Adam and Eve? Remember what got them in trouble? They started looking at what God hadn't given them instead of what he had given them, and the rest is history (literally). Contentment is the opposite of coveting. Contentment is that powerful moment when your reality and the liberating concept of *enough* embrace each other. Content people don't want more. And at the moment you decide you have *enough*, at the moment you determine that you're not pursuing anything else, you're rich.

People who covet what others have—their jobs, houses, cars, spouses, bodies, vacation homes, whatever—are never rich. It doesn't matter how much money or stuff they have; there's always that "monster of more" craving for yet another sacrifice. They're never satisfied; they never have *enough*. Don't forget the timeless teaching of Solomon: "Whoever loves money never has money enough; whoever loves wealth is never satisfied with his income. This too is meaningless" (Eccles. 5:10).

Those who are rich toward God choose joy over happiness. Happiness is an American virtue. We so value happiness

108

that we listed the pursuit of it as a right in our Declaration of Independence. But there's a problem with happiness—it's circumstantial. It's based on certain conditions. Thus your happiness may wax and wane with the levels of the stock market, the moods of your spouse, your health, the weather, or the wins and losses of your favorite sports team.

Joy, on the other hand, isn't based on circumstances. It is the fruit of knowing that your hope and future lie securely with Christ in heaven. It doesn't mean you won't have bad days or that you don't suffer. But joy always prevails. Happiness can be shattered; joy can't. Joy is the garment of those who are rich toward God. They always have it on.

There are believers around the world who are suffering for their faith in Christ. Some have had their property taken from them; some have been imprisoned; others have seen their loved ones killed—all because they follow Jesus. I doubt that many of them are happy. How could they be? But I know they have joy. The temporary pains of this world cannot snuff out their deep-rooted faith and the joy it yields. Joy enables believers to pray for and bless their persecutors. Joy will enable you to still rejoice, even in the most difficult of circumstances. And it has nothing to do with how much stuff you have.

Are you rich toward God?

On the Road Again, Part 2

Tim and Margaret knew they had made the wrong call. Even with their new level of financial security and comfort, they missed their home, their church, and their friends. Their new life in Austin wasn't bad, but it just didn't feel right.

So Tim did a very courageous thing. He called his former boss and asked for his old job back. He was honest with him and told him that he and Margaret regretted their decision to leave Ohio. The boss was thrilled and told Tim the job was there when he wanted it.

I'll never forget the Sunday that Tim walked up to me and told me they were moving home. It was such a radical move, I was blown away. Tim and Margaret immediately landed on my "Kingdom Hero" list. I respect them, not only because they had the courage to admit and correct their mistake, but also because they didn't let money be the primary drive in their decision. For them, it simply wasn't worth losing their church, family, and friends over money.

Moving Toward Enough

From Thom and Celia: Downsizing was a decision that took a long time for us to make. We had a house we loved, a good job, and no pressing reason for any change. But the more we got involved in serving, specifically in Reynosa, Mexico, the more the Lord softened our hearts to have a desire to give. We felt like we were not in a position to give as much as we wanted to because of our mortgage, bills, and projects we faced if we stayed in our "dream home." Ultimately, as God showed us the real needs in the ministries we were passionate about, fixing up our dream home didn't compare with being in a position to help them.

We found a smaller house we liked, put a contingency offer down, and then put our home on the market. We felt like if the Lord wanted us to move, he would work out all the details. And he did work them out—in just thirty days in a down market! We have found that God is a great realtor when he wants to be. Anyway, we landed in the new, smaller house, with a much smaller mortgage.

Despite the speedy sale of our home, we were sure we had made a crazy decision and we often questioned ourselves; but God blessed us in ways we would have never imagined. For example, as we were going through the process of downsizing, the company I had worked at for eighteen years was bought out and our very small stock position was suddenly worth five times as much. That blessing not only allowed us to give more, but it also put us in a position to be open to whatever the Lord might have for us. Just a few months later, out of nowhere, "whatever" happened, and we were approached about leaving the marketplace and entering full-time ministry. Had we not downsized, we would have been in no position to seriously consider the ministry opportunity.

While we obviously feel that our initial decision to downsize was really the beginning of a journey, we have to admit that the journey has not been easy. God really opened our eyes to issues we needed to face—ones that we didn't realize we had—like taking pride in our home and our concern for having others' approval. We feel that God has used this journey to draw us closer to him and prepare us for serving him even more. Every time we have stepped out in obedience, God has been faithful to provide for us. In fact, the bigger the step, the more he has blown us away.

For Further Reflection

1. Think about the concept of Decision Time. How do you know when your barns are full and when it's time to either build bigger ones or start giving things away?

2. Why do people often feel a near moral obligation to make more money, even if it means leaving family and friends and moving across the country?

3. Read Ephesians 1:3 and then make a list of the ways you feel rich and blessed by God. Try to limit the number of material blessings you list.

Less Than Enough

> *The poor and needy search for water, but there is none; their tongues are parched with thirst. But I the LORD will answer them; I, the God of Israel, will not forsake them.*
>
> Isaiah 41:17

8

Rich Man/Poor Man

Less than enough. If *enough* means that your daily needs are met, and *more than enough* means that you have provision beyond what you need at the moment, then what does it mean to have *less than enough*? It must mean that we have less than what our daily needs require. And given how little the Bible says that we really need on a daily basis, having less than that means that we have very little at all.

For many of us, having *less than enough* is a foreign concept. Personally, I've never experienced it. I need to make it practical so I can get my brain around it. Having *less than enough*, less than you need each day, might mean that:

- You don't have diapers or formula for your baby.
- You don't have health insurance and can't afford routine medical or dental care for yourself or your family.

- You can't fix your car when it breaks down, which means you might miss work.
- You can't afford to fix the leak in your roof (if you own your house), or to fix the hot water heater, the washer and/or dryer, the AC, or the refrigerator should any of them stop working.
- You might have to choose between paying the electricity bill and buying groceries.
- You might go to bed one night not knowing where tomorrow's meals are coming from.
- You typically can't afford to buy a Christmas tree, or even Christmas presents.
- When wronged—your ex-husband stops paying child support, you're hit by an uninsured driver, you're fired without cause—you can't afford to get legal help.

Millions of people live this way every day. You don't have to go to India or Central America to find people living with *less than enough*. Sometimes they're right next door.

Lazarus

Remember Thurston, the rich man that Jesus introduced us to in Luke 16? One of the reasons Jesus told us about Thurston was so he could contrast him with another man. I don't have to create a name for this second man, since Jesus tells us his name and describes him in detail: "At his [the rich man, Thurston's] gate was laid a beggar named Lazarus, covered with sores and longing to eat what fell from the rich man's table. Even the dogs came and licked his sores" (Luke 16:20–21). You need to know that I believe Thurston and Lazarus were real people. I don't believe Jesus is using a parable here. Jesus never used names in parables. The fact that Jesus tells us Lazarus' name means that this story is real, and that makes what Jesus taught about him even more profound.

Lazarus had *less than enough*. He was reduced to begging and possibly stealing just to survive. It's obvious that he wasn't getting the medical care he needed. We should also notice the proximity of Lazarus to Thurston's house. Lazarus was close enough to scavenge off of what Thurston's servants threw away. That means that Thurston probably knew of Lazarus' plight. Perhaps they had an arrangement that gave Lazarus permission to take Thurston's leftovers. But Jesus' main points seem to be that Lazarus was so poor that he needed someone else's help, and that there was very little physical distance between him and the someone who could indeed help him. And those are the points that we need to ponder as we consider what it means to have *less than enough*.

Those with *less than enough* depend on others for their daily existence. In most cases, if they could fend for themselves they would. Sure, there are a few freeloaders who would rather panhandle than work; but among the world's poor, they're the exception. You can be certain that those who are desperate enough to need someone else's help just to survive don't like living that way. They would do anything to change their circumstances. In many cases, however, there's little hope for them to break out of the vicious cultural cycle that breeds *less than enough*.

Those with *less than enough* are close by. They may be right at our doorstep. That, I think, is the most haunting part of this real-life story. Thurston obviously had the means to help Lazarus, probably at very little cost to him personally. But he didn't. For whatever reason—busyness, distraction, or just callousness—Thurston looked the other way. He felt that sharing his leftovers fulfilled any responsibility he had for Lazarus. Apparently not.

So what does that say about me? I've got clothes in my closet I haven't worn in over a year. I own multiple pairs of reading glasses, have several pairs of work boots, several coats (most of which I never wear because I live in central Texas), and food that sits for weeks or even months in my pantry. And yet the poor are all around me. Surely they could benefit from my extras. But is that really my job?

Just about the time I'm somehow able to excuse myself from owning any responsibility for those with *less than enough*, God reminds me of his truth. Today's not-so-gentle reminder came from the prophet Ezekiel: "This was the sin of your sister Sodom: She and her daughters were arrogant, overfed and unconcerned; they did not help the poor and needy" (Ezek. 16:49). Yikes! Okay, I really wish that verse wasn't in the Bible. So maybe those with *less than enough* should matter to me. How do I change my heart toward them?

Annie

Let's put a face on those with *less than enough*. Annie is a bright, articulate, motivated young woman. She's spunky, fun to be around, a hard worker, and a Christian. She also struggles daily with having *less than enough*.

According to the US Census Bureau, Annie—a single mother of two who waits tables for a living—lives just above the poverty level.[1] That means that she's only one blown transmission or one large doctor bill from dipping below it. She doesn't have insurance and struggles to stay just ahead of the financial curve. Annie doesn't look like someone you might expect to have *less than enough*. And that may be the point. We have these stereotypes—right or wrong—of what the poor look like: disheveled, unbathed, poorly educated, and not anything like us. But Annie doesn't fit any of those stereotypes. She's the girl next door—literally.

Annie does a great job of keeping her spirits up, even in the face of daily adversity. But sometimes her circumstances get the best of her. Just after a recent Thanksgiving Annie texted me. Her little boy had gotten the flu and then she had gotten sick as well. The two of them, along with her six-year-old daughter, spent Thanksgiving weekend at home alone. The planned trip to Grandma's house was cancelled. On top of that, her daughter was running low on clothes. She'd been through a growth spurt and didn't have much that fit anymore. Annie's text to me was a cry for help. She was sad, lonely, and hurting for her kids.

After a few phone calls and a couple of emails, several families in our church responded to Annie's plight. Bags and bags of clothes showed up at her workplace. Annie got back on her feet and was able to better provide for her daughter. But the significance of this story didn't hit me until later. One morning when I was dining at the restaurant where she works, Annie told me her daughter had enjoyed choosing what she would wear to school that day. She told me about how she had held up two or three outfits for her little girl, asking, "Would you rather wear this, or this, or this?" Then, with tears welling in her eyes, she told me that day was the first she could remember her little girl actually having a choice of what clothes she wanted to wear to school.

And that's when it hit home. Those with *less than enough* aren't different from me. They may or may not be unkempt or uneducated, but they're still exactly like me. They have hopes and dreams just like I do. They want the best for their kids just like I do. And when the world closes in around them, they hurt. Just like I do.

Rethinking "Less Than Enough"

Jesus was poor. That's part of the gospel message that often doesn't get preached. He was born to an impoverished family and probably never had many earthly possessions. Many Bible scholars believe that Jesus' earthly dad, Joseph, died while Jesus was still young. He isn't mentioned along with Mary after the account of Jesus in the temple at age twelve. That may mean that Jesus started working as a carpenter to help support the family while he was still relatively young.

Does knowing that Jesus was poor change how you feel about people with *less than enough*? Does it make them more personal, more approachable, more real? Have you ever thought about what being poor does to a person? I really hadn't. But when I started traveling to poor countries I quickly saw what having *less than enough* can do to individuals, families, and even nations.

Let's take just a moment and think together about the impact of living with *less than enough*. Living with *less than enough* . . .

- *Steals childhood.* Children who grow up in poverty live hard lives. They lose the opportunity to be "normal" kids. Most are forced to drop out of school (if they go at all) while still in their elementary years. They're required to either work or stay home and guard what few possessions they may have from thieves. While my ten-year-old may be trying to decide what video game to play next, his counterpart who lives in the land of *less than enough* may be trying to fight off a bandit who wants to steal a piece of cookware or a chicken.

- *Breeds addictions.* There is a very close link between living with *less than enough* and addictive behaviors. Poverty breeds despair, and despair opens the door for alcoholism, drug abuse, and sexual promiscuity. Talk to a family who lives with *less than enough* and you'll frequently find generations of addictive lifestyles.

- *Yields abuse.* With despair and addictions comes abuse as well. Physical and sexual abuse are part and parcel of chronic poverty. Most of the women we minister to in Nicaragua—young or old, married or single—have been the victims of sexual abuse.

- *Results in loss of family.* People with *less than enough* often don't live long lives. Many a child has lost one or both parents due to the ravages of poverty.

- *Produces hopelessness.* Living with *less than enough* kills dreams. Kids who might otherwise aspire to become engineers or physicians or teachers learn early that such dreams are meaningless when you're fighting just to stay alive. And since poverty is generational, breaking free from the cycle of hopelessness is next to impossible.

The Party Line

I used to be really good at writing off those with *less than enough* as "not my problem." I can justify just about anything when properly motivated. And things like resisting change or guilt are great motivators for me. Here are some of my favorite excuses (some I've used, some I've heard others use) for ignoring those with *less than enough*.

- I don't know any poor people. Everyone I know has plenty of everything. What am I supposed to do, go on a scavenger hunt for a poor person?
- All they really need is the gospel. If we get them saved and going to heaven, they'll be fine.
- I feel really bad for them. Isn't that enough? I know I can't solve all the world's problems, but at least I'm sad about their situation.
- Would a person who has lived in poverty all of his or her life really know how to manage having money or possessions? Wouldn't that be like a severe culture shock? Don't they get used to being poor?
- Aren't the poor better off than those of us with wealth? Think about it—they have fewer distractions to deal with. Plus, didn't Jesus say the poor are blessed?
- We can't solve poverty. Jesus said we'd always have the poor with us. So if even Jesus knew that we'd never solve the problem of poverty, what's the point in trying?
- If we start helping the poor, don't we just make them more dependent on us? Don't we just make them more beggarly than they already are?
- Aren't they poor because they aren't willing to work? Or isn't their poverty God's collective judgment on their

lives or their nation for their mismanagement of their opportunities?

- Look, there are just as many poor here as there are in other countries. Why should we run off to Africa when there are so many poor right here?

And for every one of these attempts to dodge dealing with the issue of *less than enough*, I found solid biblical answers. Why don't we consider a few of them?

Word

If I'm being honest, I'm amazed at how long I "overlooked" the biblical passages that teach about our responsibility toward those with *less than enough*. I mean, I knew they were in the Bible and I read them regularly; I just didn't think they applied to me. I'm grateful to my friends Cecil and Ginny Campbell of Nicaragua Resource Network (nicaresourcenet. org) for gently helping me see the Bible's call on my life as a believer to serve those with *less than enough*.

Here is just a sampling of the verses in the Bible that speak of God's care for those with *less than enough* and our responsibility to them. I've added a brief summary statement before each.

- *Leave some of what you have for those with less than enough.* "When you reap the harvest of your land, do not reap to the very edges of your field or gather the gleanings of your harvest. Do not go over your vineyard a second time or pick up the grapes that have fallen.

Leave them for the poor and the alien. I am the LORD your God" (Lev. 19:9–10).

- *Be quick to share with the needy.* "If there is a poor man among your brothers in any of the towns of the land that the LORD your God is giving you, do not be hardhearted or tightfisted toward your poor brother. Rather be openhanded and freely lend him whatever he needs" (Deut. 15:7–8).

- *Because there will always be those with less than enough, we must take the opportunity to share with them.* "There will always be poor people in the land. Therefore I command you to be openhanded toward your brothers and toward the poor and needy in your land" (Deut. 15:11).

- *God protects and defends the poor.* "I know that the LORD secures justice for the poor and upholds the cause of the needy" (Ps. 140:12).

- *God honors those who serve the poor.* "He who is kind to the poor lends to the LORD, and he will reward him for what he has done" (Prov. 19:17).

- *It honors God when we sacrifice for the benefit of others.* "Is it not to share your food with the hungry and to provide the poor wanderer with shelter—when you see the naked, to clothe him, and not to turn away from your own flesh and blood?" (Isa. 58:7).

- *You get to know God better when you serve those with less than enough.* "'Does it make you a king to have more and more cedar? Did not your father have food and drink? He did what was right and just, so all went well with him. He defended the cause of the poor and needy, and so all went well. Is that not what it means to know me?' declares the LORD" (Jer. 22:15–16).

- *When you have a banquet, make a habit of inviting those who can't return the favor.* "Then Jesus said to his host, 'When you give a luncheon or dinner, do not invite your friends, your brothers or relatives, or your rich neighbors; if you do, they may invite you back and so you will be repaid. But when you give a banquet, invite the poor, the crippled, the lame, the blind, and you will be blessed. Although they cannot repay you, you will be repaid at the resurrection of the righteous'" (Luke 14:12–14).

- *Serving those with less than enough is the same as serving Christ.* "Then the righteous will answer him, 'Lord, when did we see you hungry and feed you, or thirsty and give you something to drink? When did we see you a stranger and invite you in, or needing clothes and clothe you? When did we see you sick or in prison and go to visit you?' The King will reply, 'I tell you the truth, whatever you did for one of the least of these brothers of mine, you did for me'" (Matt. 25:37–40).

- *Jesus' mission included helping the poor.* "The Spirit of the Lord is on me, because he has anointed me to preach good news to the poor. He has sent me to proclaim freedom for the prisoners and recovery of sight for the blind, to release the oppressed, to proclaim the year of the Lord's favor" (Luke 4:18–19).

- *Pure worship includes serving the poor.* "Religion that God our Father accepts as pure and faultless is this: to look after orphans and widows in their distress and to keep oneself from being polluted by the world" (James 1:27).

- *God's love is best expressed when we serve the poor.* "If anyone has material possessions and sees his brother in need but has no pity on him, how can the love of God be in him?" (1 John 3:17).

Maybe you're thinking, "Wow, I didn't know the Bible said that." Here's something else you may not have known: there are over three hundred verses in the Bible that speak about those with *less than enough*. Three hundred! Kind of makes you wonder how we could so easily overlook them, doesn't it?

They Never Forget

During my last two years at Baylor University, I served as the pastor of a small country church about an hour from Waco, Texas. Hay Valley Baptist Church was outside of Gatesville, just ten minutes past a Texas Department of Corrections facility. About eighty to ninety people attended regularly on Sundays, unless one of the families decided to have a family reunion—then pretty much everybody was gone.

People who go to churches like Hay Valley have a special spot reserved for them in heaven. They operate on a shoestring budget, so they can only afford to hire part-time leadership. Many of them, including Hay Valley, hire students from nearby Bible schools or seminaries. They give young ministers the chance to learn to preach, marry, bury, baptize, counsel, and do just about anything else that a little church requires. It's a great ministry to young pastors, and the people show great patience and tolerance as they sit through any number of really bad sermons, muffed weddings, and forgotten names at funerals. I know, because I did my share of muffing at Hay Valley.

The generous folks at Hay Valley hired me to preach Sundays and Wednesdays and agreed to pay me $60 a week. I was thrilled; I was also rich. After about three months, they decided I had potential and gave me a raise—all the way up to $75 a week. I couldn't believe it. This preaching gig was a financial windfall! Seventy-five bucks a week is pretty high cotton for a kid in college, at least it was in 1983.

I remember calling my dad and telling him about the raise. I knew that he would be both impressed and excited for me. The conversation went something like this:

ME: Hey Dad, guess what? I got a raise!

DAD: A raise? Really? Didn't they just hire you?

ME: Yep, and they like me. That's why they increased my salary.

DAD: Will, it's not really a salary. You don't work enough to call it a salary. How much are you making?

ME: Seventy-five dollars a week! They gave me a fifteen-dollar-a-week raise after only three months!

DAD: Seventy-five dollars a week? So they're paying you $3,900 a year?

ME: Yep. I guess that's right.

DAD: (and I'll never forget this line) Congratulations, Son. You're $6,000 *below* the poverty line.

My dad and I still laugh about that conversation.

Was my dad being hard on me? No. Was he trying to discourage me? Certainly not. My dad was and still is very proud of me. As I mentioned earlier, my dad grew up poor, very poor. He was the only child of his single mother. She worked long and hard hours to provide for them both. My dad started working at age nine, maybe earlier. At the time of this writing, he's eighty-one years old and still working. He's an accomplished attorney who has had great financial success, but he doesn't really want to quit. Why? Once you've been poor, you never forget it. No matter how successful you become, the hounds of *less than enough* are always nipping at your heels. So when my dad saw me choose a career path that isn't known for high financial reward, well, let's just say he was a little skeptical. And my days at Hay Valley, regardless of how good the church was to me, didn't do much to diminish his concerns.

It isn't fun to be poor. Few people choose to be. But many people around the world—and some right next door—can't break out of their *less than enough* cycle because of the strongholds of things like illiteracy, drug and alcohol abuse, and government leaders who want to keep the poor dependent on them. Fortunately, through his hard work and God's grace, my dad was able to break out of that cycle. Many can't; and today, even as you're reading these words, they're living with *less than enough*.

Moving Toward Enough

From Julie: I just recently finished a ten-day fast. It included many disciplines, such as:

- No watching television
- Only listening to Christian music
- Only eating certain foods
- On one day of the fast I could only eat broth
- I had to abstain from all "me spending." That meant no getting my nails done, no new clothes, etc.

It was amazing what was revealed to me. I kept a journal through the process and wrote down the things that I think God has been trying to say to me for years. It took me living with less for ten days to realize the abundance God has planned for me.

For Further Reflection

1. Do you know someone who is currently living with *less than enough*? A friend, relative, co-worker, or maybe even you? How do you think people feel who have to look to others for help just so they can get through a day?
2. Read Luke 10:29–37 and list some of your "neighbors" whom God may want you to serve.
3. Read Luke 4:16–21 and meditate on why Jesus included serving the poor as part of his personal mission.

9

What Does the Lord Require?

justice (noun): 1. the maintenance or administration of what is just, especially by the impartial adjustment of conflicting claims or the assignment of merited rewards or punishments; 2. the administration of law; *especially*: the establishment or determination of rights according to the rules of law or equity; 3. the quality of being just, impartial, or fair; 4. conformity to truth, fact, or reason.[1]

Bismark

I met Bismark several years ago. He was probably four or five years old at the time. I'll never forget seeing him for the first time. He was wearing a Home Depot employee apron that was way too big for him. His right arm was wrapped in a makeshift cast that was unraveling. And he had one of the brightest smiles I'd ever seen. The fact that he lived in an orphanage in a poor country hadn't dampened his spirits one bit, at least on the surface. Bismark was vivacious, outgoing, and fun loving. I spent the better part of a day with Bismark on my shoulders, letting him shoot baskets from the much more advantageous position of being a couple of feet below the rim. (Trust me, it took my neck and shoulders a few days to forgive me for that day's fun with Bismark.)

Bismark lived in the orphanage with his adorable younger sister, Margarita, and his older brother, Felix. I don't know how they got there. Their parents more than likely abandoned them simply because they couldn't afford to raise them. Unfortunately that is a common effect of poverty—parents often just abandon their children out of sheer despair and/or desperation. But the kids had a decent life in the orphanage. They had three meals a day, they were receiving a great education, and they were surrounded by adults who loved them and cared for them.

I quickly learned that Bismark, Felix, and Margarita were atypical. The blessing of a Christian orphanage for these three is the exception, not the rule. Most of the world's orphans know no such good fortune. They're unfed, unclothed, uneducated, and most tragically, they're often unloved. Theirs is a misery that few of us will ever know or comprehend.

It is not a misery, however, that we get to ignore. The Bible calls us to become the voice of the voiceless and the defenders of the defenseless. Those of us with *more than enough* get to step into the worlds of those with *less than enough* and be their voice, their advocates, and their friends.

I would also soon learn that the safety afforded Bismark and his siblings was tenuous at best. Things can change overnight for an orphan, even those as well cared for as Bismark.

Justice

The Bible has much to say about justice. By my count, the New International Version uses the English word over 130 times. Only sixteen of those occurrences are in the New Testament. But the justice that dominates the pages of Scripture may not be the same as the justice you're thinking of. Our culture has conditioned us to think of justice as the appropriate judgment and recompense of wrongs. It's payback for the criminals and, when possible, the restoration of what the victim has lost. We call it justice when a child molester gets life in prison or when a factory worker who was injured by his employer's malfeasance gets financial compensation. And both are indeed examples of justice.

But the concept of biblical justice goes much further. God does indeed call for the punishment of the guilty and restitution for the wronged, but he also calls his people to actively pursue justice for those who cannot pursue it for themselves. In fact, God commands his people to be the justice advocates for the poor and needy. Consider the following:

- "Good will come to him who is generous and lends freely, who conducts his affairs with justice" (Ps. 112:5).
- "I know that the LORD secures justice for the poor and upholds the cause of the needy" (Ps. 140:12).
- "The righteous care about justice for the poor, but the wicked have no such concern" (Prov. 29:7).

- "Stop doing wrong, learn to do right! Seek justice, encourage the oppressed. Defend the cause of the fatherless, plead the case of the widow" (Isa. 1:16–17).

- "Woe to those who make unjust laws, to those who issue oppressive decrees, to deprive the poor of their rights and withhold justice from the oppressed of my people, making widows their prey and robbing the fatherless" (Isa. 10:1–2).

- "This is what the LORD says: 'Let not the wise man boast of his wisdom or the strong man boast of his strength or the rich man boast of his riches, but let him who boasts boast about this: that he understands and knows me, that I am the LORD, who exercises kindness, justice and righteousness on earth, for in these I delight,' declares the LORD" (Jer. 9:23–24).

- "The people of the land practice extortion and commit robbery; they oppress the poor and needy and mistreat the alien, denying them justice" (Ezek. 22:29).

- "And the word of the LORD came again to Zechariah: 'This is what the LORD Almighty says: "Administer true justice; show mercy and compassion to one another"'" (Zech. 7:8–9).

- "Woe to you, teachers of the law and Pharisees, you hypocrites! You give a tenth of your spices—mint, dill and cumin. But you have neglected the more important matters of the law—justice, mercy and faithfulness. You should have practiced the latter, without neglecting the former" (Matt. 23:23).

If you're new to the Bible, you might be surprised by its emphasis on justice, and specifically its emphasis on justice

134

for those who can't get it for themselves. Again, it seems that God intends for his people to be ambassadors of justice on earth and that the groups we should speak most loudly for are those who cannot speak for themselves.

The Armadillo

The Hill Country west of Austin is filled with gorgeous lakes, beautiful rolling hills, and breathtaking panoramas. The Texas Hill Country is a rare jewel in a state known for its flat farmland and rugged ranchland. As a result, the property values in the hills west of Austin are quite high and the half-acre lots in the area boast $1 million to $3 million homes.

Then there's the Armadillo. The Armadillo RV Park is about two acres of poverty that sits right in the middle of one of the more affluent parts of the Lake Travis region of the Austin Hill Country. The Armadillo is home to about thirty families—some Spanish-speaking, some English-speaking, all poor. The RVs they live in tend to add to the collective misery of the area: they're run-down, broken, damaged, leaky, and, in some cases, unsafe.

Some of the most beautiful children I've ever seen live in the Armadillo. I'm not sure what it is about kids who live in poverty that makes them so adorable—maybe it's their bright eyes, unquenchable spirits, or the automatic sympathy and compassion you feel for them—but once you meet them, you're hooked. They don't seem to know they're poor, at least not yet. But when you look into the eyes of their parents, you get a different feeling. Their eyes tell a different story. You can see the pain and stress—the inadequate medical care, the nagging hunger, the uncertain future—that slowly dampens the light in their eyes. They do have one thing in common with their kids—once you meet them, you don't forget them either.

The Armadillo—its residents and their living conditions—is one big, ugly oxymoron for the area. I mean, just a six-iron shot away from the Armadillo are some of the largest, most luxurious homes in central Texas. The families that live in those homes are blessed with air-conditioning, hot and cold (and clean) running water, education and travel opportunities, and the ability to pursue their dreams. They have some of the best health care in the world, and they eat at least three good meals a day. And there's nothing wrong with how they live. They're not wrong for having *more than enough*. It's just a curious juxtaposition that so close to them are families who live on the completely opposite end of the social spectrum.

A busy road runs past the Armadillo. It comes off of a major scenic highway and leads to some of the gorgeous neighborhoods and marinas that line the shores of Lake Travis. And even though it's such an eyesore for the area, the Armadillo is still easy to miss. It's that small and insignificant.

My point is that thousands of cars pass the Armadillo every day, but few ever turn into it. And here's the question I'm struggling with: what would the concept of biblical justice have to say about that? Is God okay with the fact that such economic disparity exists in the area? As a pastor of a nearby church, what is my responsibility to the folks at the Armadillo? None of my church members live there. So do we have an obligation to help them? And what about the believers who live in the area and drive by the Armadillo every day? Do they have a responsibility to do something, and if so, what?

Bismark, Part 2

Not long ago, government officials decided that Bismark, Margarita, and Felix needed to live with their grandmother and not in the Christian orphanage where they were living. On the surface that sounds pretty reasonable. But there's much more to the story: the government doesn't want kids growing up either educated or Christian. They want them poor, uneducated, and without a worldview that tells them they should work for something greater than just their own survival. Stated more directly, the government leaders want a populace that is dependent on them. So they take every opportunity to move kids out of settings that might produce young men and women who could someday threaten their status quo.

The other detail of the story is that Bismark's grandmother lived in a dump—literally. An entire community and social structure exists in the city dump—which was at one time home to more than ten thousand people. The people who live there battle the dogs, vultures, and sometimes each other for the few scraps of food that are brought in each day.

One of the words the Bible uses for hell is the name of a dump that existed outside of Jerusalem. After seeing the dump where Bismark lived, I clearly understood why the biblical writers connected a dump to a place of torment and suffering. This one was terrible. Some people are born into the dump and literally spend their entire lives there. And for some reason, government officials felt that Bismark, Margarita, and Felix would be better off there in the dump than in the loving environment they knew in the orphanage.

A few months after Bismark and his siblings were taken to the dump, Bismark lost his footing while playing near a drainage ditch during a rainstorm. Felix, who had been playing with him, tried to grab Bismark, and both fell into the rushing water. Their bodies were found a few days later, miles away in Lake Managua.

Is that justice? I think we'd all agree that this is a terrible miscarriage of justice. But in reality, there is very little we could have done to protect Bismark. Our church and others are working with local Christian leaders on a long-term strategy to change that nation, but the immediate risk and potential for injustice is still high. So where do we draw the line? If God expects his people to be the hands and feet of his justice, then what does that mean practically? How far do we go? What are those of us with *more than enough* really required to do for those with *less than enough*?

Justice, Part 2

Actually, we find a reasonable answer to the question "what is required of us?" in the Old Testament. The prophet Micah is well known for giving us one of the best summary statements about justice in the Bible. He wrote, "He has showed you, O man, what is good. And what does the LORD require of you? To act justly and to love mercy and to walk humbly with your God" (Micah 6:8).

Prophets like Micah, who ministered to Judah and Israel in the eighth century BC, were up against a cultural backdrop of oppression and abuse of the poor. The rich not only didn't help the poor, they exploited them. Judges offered decisions based not on what was right and just, but based on who paid them the highest bribe. Religious leaders and "prophets" were swayed by whoever could give them the greatest perks, not by what they heard God's Spirit saying. As a result, prophets like Amos, Micah, Isaiah, Jeremiah, and Hosea rebuked the nations for their neglect of the poor and for openly disregarding God's commands to be the promoters of justice in the world.

Micah 6:8 sums up these prophets' collective sentiments quite nicely. What does God want? *Do justice.* It's hard to miss the beautiful simplicity of that message. As far as it is up to us, when we have the means and access to promote justice or to reverse injustice for someone around us, then we need to do it. Writing some eight centuries after Micah, James, the half brother of Jesus, said it this way: "Anyone, then, who knows the good he ought to do and doesn't do it, sins" (James 4:17).

So what does God expect of us? How can those of us with *more than enough* serve those with *less than enough*?

- *Open your eyes.* Let's be aware of the needs around us. Don't be in such a hurry that you don't really see what's going on down the street or around the world.
- *Pray for opportunities.* Ask God to give you opportunities to provide justice for someone who needs it.
- *Protect margin.* Keep some time open and resources available so that when God brings you a need, you'll be able to meet it.
- *Speak for those who can't speak for themselves.* People groups like the unborn, special needs kids and adults, orphans, shut-ins, people suffering from HIV/AIDS, former prostitutes, prison inmates, and ex-felons have very few advocates in the world, and even fewer in the church. Find a group that you feel passionate about and

start serving them and doing what you can to protect them or to improve their plight.

- *Enlist.* Fighting for justice isn't what zealots do; it's part and parcel of God's call on our lives. Embrace the biblical reality that part of why you're here on earth is to lighten the load of others.

Moving Toward Enough

Redirect rental income. A couple in our church owns some rental property. Instead of collecting rent from the tenants, they ask them to give the same amount to a ministry or nonprofit. The couple provides a list of ministries they have vetted and that they support, and then they let the renters decide whom they want to give to. It's a win for everyone: the tenants get a tax deduction, the owners help teach giving, stewardship, and promoting justice, and the ministry gets additional funds.

For Further Reflection

1. Read Isaiah 58:6–10 and list some ways that God's view of justice may be broader than our contemporary view of justice.
2. With so many tragic stories like Bismark's happening around the world every day, how can we have any serious impact? List three to five things you could do today that would help someone like Bismark.
3. Memorize Micah 6:8 and ask God to help you to "do justice" on a daily basis.

Moving Toward Enough

All the believers were together and had everything in common. Selling their posses-sions and goods, they gave to anyone as he had need.

Acts 2:44–45

10

World-Class Christianity

world-class (adj.): being of the highest caliber in
the world, i.e., a *world-class* athlete.[1]

I've always wondered if I could have been a world-class athlete. I was a pretty good competitive water skier as a kid, but
a severely injured ankle one summer ended all that. I loved
running track and was a decent overall athlete, so maybe I
could have been a decathlete. But world-class? I don't think so.

So then I wonder, am I a world-class anything? Is there
a hobby, a skill, or a profession, some discipline in which I
might be considered to set the standard? Again, probably not.
My skills and talents just aren't that exceptional. But what
about faith? I'm a serious Christ-follower. I'm certainly not
perfect, but I'm not playing games either. I mean business
in my walk with Christ and I try to leverage my life as best I
can for God's kingdom. So how do I stack up against other
believers around the world and throughout history? Am I
carrying my weight? I know I'm not competing with other

Jesus-followers, but how am I doing on a world scale? Who sets the standard of excellence for Christians?

If there is such a thing as a world-class Christian, how do we know what it is? And how do we adhere to such a vigorous standard? Well, we don't have to wonder. The Bible tells us.

What Makes a World-Class Christian?

What is the international gold standard for Christianity? Where is the bar of faith set at its highest point? One might offer many suggestions:

- *Giving.* Surely those who give generously set the bar for the rest of us.
- *Prayer.* Intercession moves mountains, so intercessors must be world-class Christians.
- *Evangelism.* It's hard to top the impact of helping to bring a new soul into the kingdom.
- *Missions.* Those who embrace a different culture for the sake of the gospel are surely standouts in God's kingdom.

All of these are great suggestions, and all have their place in serious Christ-following. But none are what the Bible points to as the highest level of commitment to Christ. None carry the true badge of honor bestowed on only a certain class of Christian. So what is it? What does the Bible establish as the world-class standard for Christ-following? In a word, *suffering*. The highest level of commitment to Christ belongs to those who endure chronic suffering and yet remain faithful to him in the process.

That's right, the pinnacle of Christian living to which we all must aspire isn't honor, but dishonor; not comfort, but discomfort; not fame, but obscurity.

Okay, let's all say it together: "Ouch."

Skeptical? Let's let the Bible speak for itself:

- "Blessed are those who are persecuted because of righteousness, for theirs is the kingdom of heaven" (Matt. 5:10).
- "The apostles left the Sanhedrin, rejoicing because they had been counted worthy of suffering disgrace for the Name" (Acts 5:41).
- "But the Lord said to Ananias [about Paul], 'Go! This man is my chosen instrument to carry my name before the Gentiles and their kings and before the people of Israel. I will show him how much he must suffer for my name'" (Acts 9:15–16).
- "For it has been granted to you on behalf of Christ not only to believe on him, but also to suffer for him" (Phil. 1:29).
- "I want to know Christ and the power of his resurrection and the fellowship of sharing in his sufferings . . ." (Phil. 3:10).
- "All this is evidence that God's judgment is right, and as a result you will be counted worthy of the kingdom of God, for which you are suffering" (2 Thess. 1:5).
- "So do not be ashamed to testify about our Lord, or ashamed of me his prisoner. But join with me in suffering for the gospel, by the power of God" (2 Tim. 1:8).

145

- "The brother in humble circumstances ought to take pride in his high position. But the one who is rich should take pride in his low position, because he will pass away like a wild flower" (James 1:9–10).

- "Brothers, as an example of patience in the face of suffering, take the prophets who spoke in the name of the Lord" (James 5:10).

- "But how is it to your credit if you receive a beating for doing wrong and endure it? But if you suffer for doing good and you endure it, this is commendable before God. To this you were called, because Christ suffered for you, leaving you an example, that you should follow in his steps" (1 Pet. 2:20–21).

- "But even if you should suffer for what is right, you are blessed. 'Do not fear what they fear; do not be frightened'" (1 Pet. 3:14).

- "Therefore, since Christ suffered in his body, arm yourselves also with the same attitude, because he who has suffered in his body is done with sin" (1 Pet. 4:1).

- "However, if you suffer as a Christian, do not be ashamed, but praise God that you bear that name" (1 Pet. 4:16).

- "So then, those who suffer according to God's will should commit themselves to their faithful Creator and continue to do good" (1 Pet. 4:19).

- "I, John, your brother and companion in the suffering and kingdom and patient endurance that are ours in Jesus, was on the island of Patmos because of the word of God and the testimony of Jesus" (Rev. 1:9).

- "Do not be afraid of what you are about to suffer. I tell you, the devil will put some of you in prison to test you, and you will suffer persecution for ten days. Be faithful, even to the point of death, and I will give you the crown of life" (Rev. 2:10).

Yes, I know. Those verses are a real buzzkill. Welcome to world-class Christianity. Better yet, welcome to biblical Christianity.

Suffering 101

I've got to be honest with you, I don't think I've ever really suffered. Yes, I've had bad days and difficult seasons. I've buried family members and close friends. I've had to look loved ones in the face and seek their forgiveness for my wrongs. But I've never gone to bed hungry or wondering about where my next meal will come from. I've never feared for my life (excluding a few self-inflicted close calls in the mountains), had to battle a prolonged illness, or been persecuted for my faith. I've never even had to face extended periods of physical pain. So when the Bible says that the highest standard for Christianity is suffering, I have to confess that I don't have any real idea what it's talking about. And if I hope to somehow attain to such a level of honor in the Christian faith, then I need to get my brain around what it is and isn't.

Suffering, according to the Bible, is not:

- *Being punished for doing something wrong.* When you get in trouble and suffer for it, that's not the kind of suffering that the Bible exalts. Getting a ticket, going to jail, having to do community service, paying a fine, or losing your job due to your own negligence isn't really suffering; it's justice.

- *Consequences for actions.* If your marriage is suffering because of your infidelity, that's not the kind of suffering the biblical writers esteemed. Having to spend time in a drug rehab or having to work through the difficulty of a strained relationship may be good for you and hopefully you learn from it; but experiencing pain for your bad choices isn't exactly a noble form of suffering.

- *Having a cross you must bear.* Don't get me started on this one. God doesn't assign crosses for people to bear. For more on this, see chapter 11 in my book *Ten Things Jesus Never Said.*

A little over fifteen years ago, when I was just over thirty, my body started breaking down. I'm not sure why—I mean, beyond the obvious thirty years of playing really hard. But my body started rebelling and giving me a little payback for all the years of climbing, jumping, and falling I'd made it endure. Since then, I've had four knee operations, three shoulder operations, one neck operation, and one lower back operation. I like to tell people that I'm on my way to heaven . . . I'm just going one limb at a time.

I have consistent pain in my knees and often have to take some type of painkiller at night so I can lie still enough to fall asleep. And yes, there are times I get discouraged, become grumpy, and start to feel sorry for myself. I also get tired of all the jokes and barbs made at the expense of my physical failings. But just about the time I want to be the guest of honor at my own pity party, God gives me a good dose of reality. I'm not suffering, not even close.

Having now seen what biblical suffering isn't, let's see what it is.

Simply put, suffering is prolonged physical, mental, or emotional pain, or some combination thereof, resulting from circumstances beyond your control or as the direct result of another person's actions. Consider these forms of suffering:

- *Poverty.* Prolonged living with *less than enough* clearly leads to suffering on multiple levels. The ripple effects of poverty include despair and depression, alcohol and drug abuse, physical and sexual abuse, malnutrition and other serious health issues. I can see countless faces in my mind's eye right now of people who I know woke up today in great suffering because of poverty.

- *Persecution.* This is the type of pain that comes from being attacked for one's beliefs or moral stances, and it's happening all over the world. Whether it's the whistle-blower who loses his job for pointing out unethical practices within the company, or the pastor in a foreign country who's arrested for performing a Christian wedding, or those who suffer rape, torture, and the confiscation of their property because of their Christian faith, persecution is a major source of suffering in the world today.

- *Chronic illness.* I've seen this one up close and personal, and I've seen it more than once. For whatever reason, a person gets sick—really sick, painfully sick. He or she endures years of symptoms, treatments, setbacks, more symptoms, more treatments, and even more setbacks. And yet throughout that terrible process and in all those years of suffering, he or she never loses joy. Such people live inspiring lives even while facing terrible pain and even death due to illness.

- *Natural disasters.* Earthquakes, tsunamis, hurricanes, famines (both the natural kind and those brought on by dictatorial governments), tornadoes, and the like leave a trail of human devastation in their path. When Hurricane Katrina hit the US Gulf Coast in 2005, and when a series of deadly tornadoes devastated several American towns and cities in the spring of 2011, many of us saw firsthand the type of suffering such disasters leave behind. In some cases, the pain of human and property loss still lingers today. And on the world scale, these were relatively small disasters. Who can fathom the amount of pain endured after tsunamis, earthquakes, or cyclones devastate entire nations?

- *War.* There are many victims in war, and they all suffer terribly. We see them every day in news videos and internet pictures from war-torn areas. Civilians are caught in the cross fire. Citizens of towns and villages have their homes and livelihoods destroyed by the bombs and missiles of battle. A woman sees her young child killed instantly by a stray bullet. Young men and women go off to battle, many of them never to return, and leave behind wives, children, parents, and friends. And millions and millions of people suffer terribly and live in fear, sometimes for decades, while their vicious and oppressive leaders live in luxury.

- *Great personal tragedy and loss.* I have two friends who buried their beautiful daughter recently after a yearlong battle with cancer. It was a terrible, brutal ordeal for them. I have a church member who was recently attacked

150

and violently raped. Such tragedies don't just go away for those who endure them. They mark you and change you for the rest of your life.

There are certainly other forms of suffering that we have to contend with in life. But as I looked at the list above and thought about my own life, I came to the humbling realization that I didn't really know much about suffering. I mean, rooting for a sports team that perennially has losing seasons isn't really suffering. And once I realized that I didn't know very much about suffering, I had the even more humbling realization that many people around me know it all too well.

Then I had to ask the troubling question: If suffering is the highest level of one's walk with Christ, if suffering is the gold standard for the faith, and if I, for whatever reason, don't know squat about suffering, then how can I ever come to know anything about world-class Christianity? Am I disqualified from true intimacy with Christ because I don't suffer? That question really started to bother me.

The Other S Word

If suffering represents the highest level of commitment to Christ and yields the deepest levels of intimacy with Christ, and if we're not suffering, then are we doomed to a life of mediocre Christ-following? If suffering is the true historical and biblical hallmark of world-class Christianity, and if God's assignment on my life (at least so far) doesn't include suffering, then how am I to become a world-class Christian?

There is a way. For those of us in Christ's body who are not given the opportunity to suffer for or with him, God has provided a grand and glorious means by which he may transform us into the same mettle as the suffering members. In a word, it's *sacrifice*. The non-suffering Christian's response to those who suffer for and with Christ is to join them through radical, personal sacrifice.

What is sacrifice? Webster defines the verb as "to suffer loss of, give up, renounce, injure, or destroy especially for an ideal, belief, or end."[2] Biblically, sacrifice includes the idea of doing more than what's expected, or of voluntarily reducing one's status or releasing one's resources to the degree that it costs you personally. It's voluntarily and joyfully denying your own opportunities and perceived rights for the benefit of another or simply for the glory of God. Sacrifice never refers to the releasing of surplus; it speaks instead of the releasing of what's needed. It's not giving only what you can afford; it's giving what you can't afford. It hurts you, it humbles you, and it allows you to willingly step up to the plate and join those brothers and sisters around the world who are suffering in their plight.

Consider these biblical calls to meet others' suffering with our sacrifice. (I've added a bit of my own commentary after each.)

- "If one part suffers, every part suffers with it; if one part is honored, every part rejoices with it" (1 Cor. 12:26). As members of Christ's body, we don't get to look the other way when part of the body is hurting. We need to suffer with them.
- "Now I want you to know, dear brothers and sisters, what God in his kindness has done through the churches in Macedonia. They are being tested by many troubles,

and they are very poor. But they are also filled with abundant joy, which has overflowed in rich generosity. For I can testify that they gave not only what they could afford, but far more. And they did it of their own free will. They begged us again and again for the privilege of sharing in the gift for the believers in Jerusalem. They even did more than we had hoped, for their first action was to give themselves to the Lord and to us, just as God wanted them to do" (2 Cor. 8:1–5 NLT). Paul encourages us to follow the example of the believers in Macedonia, who begged for the opportunity to give sacrificially to the Jerusalem church even though they themselves were also suffering.

- "Remember those in prison as if you were their fellow prisoners, and those who are mistreated as if you yourselves were suffering" (Heb. 13:3). Embracing the pain of our suffering brothers and sisters is our duty.

I have to admit, this is humbling stuff. I don't often think of someone else's pain as being my problem, much less of having the responsibility to sacrifice so I can share their suffering. Why would I want to? What's my motivation? It's their problem, not mine.

And therein lies the real issue: in Christ-following, we're all one body. We have to lose our "us-them" mind-set. In the body of Christ, there is no *us* and *them*—there's only us.

Uriah

If you recognize the name of Uriah the Hittite, it's probably because you know the Old Testament story of David and Bathsheba (see 2 Samuel 11). Uriah was one of David's mighty men, which means he was a very skilled warrior and was fiercely loyal to David. One time while Uriah was off with David's army fighting for his kingdom, David (who had stayed behind) seduced Uriah's wife, Bathsheba, and slept with her. After discovering that Bathsheba was pregnant, David tried to cover it up by bringing Uriah home from the battlefront to be with his wife. When that plan failed, David ordered his general to have Uriah placed at the most intense point of battle, where he was eventually killed.

It's a tragic story, and it cost David and Bathsheba dearly. Uriah, however, needs to be remembered as more than Bathsheba's unfortunate, murdered husband. He is, indeed, far more. Uriah is one of the first and best biblical examples of someone living out the "suffering versus sacrifice" principle.

When David brought Uriah home from the front lines of war, he hoped that Uriah would go home and sleep with his wife. After two failed attempts to get Uriah to do so, David finally asked Uriah why he wouldn't take advantage of his time at home and enjoy a little romantic R & R. Uriah's response is amazing: "The ark and Israel and Judah are staying in tents, and my master Joab and my lord's men are camped in the open fields. How could I go to my house to eat and drink and lie with my wife? As surely as you live, I will not do such a thing!" (2 Sam. 11:11).

I've got to be honest here: if given the same opportunity, I'm not sure I'd be so noble as Uriah. I mean, seriously? I've got the opportunity to spend a quiet night alone with Susie and, on top of that, the king wants me to? Where do I sign? But for Uriah it was unthinkable to enjoy the pleasures of being at home while his buddies and, most importantly, the ark of the covenant were in harm's way. He would never allow himself to indulge his appetites while his fellow Israelites were suffering.

That is what the suffering versus sacrifice principle looks like when lived out. It's not only choosing to deny yourself what is rightfully yours; it's also refusing what would be considered normal for you to partake of or participate in for the sake of others who don't have access to the same privileges. Uriah's philosophy of life was a far cry from our culture's "every man for himself" mind-set. For Uriah, if his brothers were suffering, then he was going to suffer too.

That's the suffering versus sacrifice principle; that's world-class Christianity.

Missing the Shot to Make the Point

Johntell Franklin was a senior in high school when his mother, Carlitha, died after a five-year battle with cancer. Johntell was also a senior leader on his Milwaukee Madison High School's basketball team, and on the day of his mother's death they were playing their out-of-state rivals, DeKalb High School.

There was a somber mood in the gymnasium as the teams prepped for the game. Players, coaches, and fans from both schools knew of Johntell's loss, and his absence in the arena was quite noticeable. But then, during the second quarter of the game, Johntell walked into the gym. When he did, both sides—fans, players, everybody—stood to applaud. It was an inspiring scene. Johntell had simply wanted to be with his friends and support his team. He wasn't ready for the outpouring of love and sympathy that he received.

Johntell asked his coach if he could play in the rest of the game. The coach quickly agreed, saying that if Johntell was up to it, he'd be thrilled to let him play. However, there was one issue: because Johntell's name had not been submitted on the pregame roster, his team would be penalized for his late arrival. The opposing team, DeKalb, would be given two technical foul free throws. And in the close battle between these two rivals, two extra points might be the margin of victory. For several minutes the coaches from both teams argued with the refs about the penalty. The refs were sympathetic but couldn't bend the rules. The penalty shots had to be taken.

Then, an amazing thing happened. DeKalb senior Darius McNeal stepped forward and offered to take the shots for his team. He, like everyone else in the room, knew why Johntell had been late to the game. He also knew that the game couldn't go on until the shots were taken. So he told his coach he would be willing to take them.

Silence fell on the gym as Darius stepped to the free throw line, completely alone. All eyes were on him as the fans, players, and coaches waited to see how this drama would play out. Darius lined up his first shot and then simply dropped the ball a few feet out in front of him. He had deliberately missed. The ref handed him the ball for his second shot, and when Darius repeated the action, the gymnasium erupted in applause and cheers. Darius and his teammates had shown a level of sportsmanship and respect for a competitor that few people of any age understand these days. And what did Darius think of all the hoopla? He brushed it off: "I did it for the guy who lost his mom. It was the right thing to do. Any one of my teammates would have done the same thing, and I think anyone on the Madison team would have done the same for us."[3]

That story still gives me goose bumps . . . and perspective.

The suffering versus sacrifice principle calls us to not take our shots when we could. It reminds us that all around the world and right next door people are suffering. Many are our brothers and sisters in Christ; others are the poor and oppressed whom Jesus commanded us to serve. For us—no, for me to live as if they don't exist is inexcusable. For me to go on with my comfy life; for me to use and consume, as if no one around me needed the things I treat so casually and even throw away; for me to be preoccupied with my well-being, pleasure, and comfort while people all around me are suffering terribly; for me to take my shots and score my points at the expense or neglect of others—well, it mocks the very Savior who sacrificed himself for me.

I'll let you decide how it applies to you.

Embracing Sacrifice

Sacrifice doesn't come naturally, at least not for me. I'd love to tell you that I'm always first to offer up my seat to someone who needs it, or that I'm quick to write checks or share goods when I see a need. But I'm not. My self-promotion and self-preservation instincts have yet to reach the point of being fully sanctified. So I need some help. I need some disciplines. I need some stimuli to help me see the fruit of my sacrifice. Here are some ways I've tried to build a sacrificial mind-set into my life.

First of all, *I pray about it.* The best and most lasting changes are those that come from the inside out. I can learn to sacrifice by forcing myself to do so, but it's much less of a battle if my heart wants to sacrifice. The Holy Spirit is God's inside-out change agent, and he responds to prayer.[4] So talk to God about your heart. Talk to God about your desire, or lack thereof, to sacrifice.

Ask God to open your eyes to the needs around you. Pray that you'll hold your gifts, skills, and resources loosely and that you'll see why you have *more than enough*. Pray for a generous heart and a compassionate spirit. Ask God to show you very specifically what he would have you release. Ask him to show you what you should sacrifice for others and then to give you the heart to do so.

Second, *I remind myself of the biblical definitions of provision and contentment*. It's easy for me to forget how much *more than enough* I really have. It's equally easy for me to be jealous of those who have more *more than enough* than I do. I have to push back against such narrow thinking by meditating on Scriptures that remind me of what's real and of exactly how much I do and don't need. Here are just a few:

- "But godliness with contentment is great gain. For we brought nothing into the world, and we can take nothing out of it. But if we have food and clothing, we will be content with that" (1 Tim. 6:6–8).
- "I know what it is to be in need, and I know what it is to have plenty. I have learned the secret of being content in any and every situation, whether well fed or hungry, whether living in plenty or in want. I can do everything through him who gives me strength" (Phil. 4:12–13).
- "Command those who are rich in this present world not to be arrogant nor to put their hope in wealth, which is

so uncertain, but to put their hope in God, who richly provides us with everything for our enjoyment. Command them to do good, to be rich in good deeds, and to be generous and willing to share. In this way they will lay up treasure for themselves as a firm foundation for the coming age, so that they may take hold of the life that is truly life" (1 Tim. 6:17–19).

One final thing I do to help develop a sacrificial mind-set is *I stay connected to those who suffer.* I have to be very deliberate about this. Several times a year I force myself to step into a setting where I know I'm going to be up close and personal with suffering people. I have plenty of opportunities in my hometown and through missions to get to know people who really do suffer. Did you see what I said there? I get to know them. I know their names and stories. I can recall their faces in my memory. And when they get personal, when they move from being statistics to people I care for, my hesitations about sacrifice evaporate. I want to serve them; I want to help them; I want to ease their suffering.

Here are some specific things you can do to stay well acquainted with those who suffer:

- Regularly visit a nursing home. Serve with Meals on Wheels or similar programs and get into the homes of shut-ins.
- Spend time with special needs children and adults. Many state and nonprofit programs need volunteers. The time with these amazing people will change you.
- Serve the homeless. There's probably a soup kitchen or a homeless shelter not far from you. Get to know

the name and story of a homeless person. You may be surprised what you find.

- Adopt an impoverished area in your city and serve there regularly. Know the name and story of someone who lives in poverty.

- Visit a third world country. I really believe that every Christian should do this at least once a year. I can do a year's worth of intense discipleship with a person in just five to seven days in a third world setting. It's not that expensive and it's not just for missionaries. It will show you what's real.

After I've spent some time in a nursing home or with some special needs adults or in a third world country, I often lie awake at night and think about how I'm living. I listen to the gentle hum of the air conditioner as I snuggle down deep in my king-size bed, having earlier enjoyed a delicious meal—for the third time that day.

And then I think about the families I served who were lined up to be given one meal—families who lived in a garbage dump. I remember my friends who (when they get work) go to construction sites in flip-flops because they can't afford shoes. I think about the children who live in an orphanage, wondering if anyone really cares about them. I think about the senior adult with Alzheimer's who spends every day of her life living with strangers. I remember that homeless camp I drive by every day and wonder how they're faring on a cold night. And when I allow myself to think about those people, when I see their faces, remember their names, and recall their stories, then suddenly my wants and needs no longer matter. Sacrifice becomes second nature. It's the least I can do. I may never suffer, but I can sacrifice. Thank God I can.

Moving Toward Enough

From Jackie: I buy a gift card at the grocery store at the beginning of each month and put $200 credit on it. Then I use it for all my shopping that month. I don't let myself cheat and spend anything else for my groceries. That way I limit my grocery spending and have more money for other, more important things.

For Further Reflection

1. Read and meditate on Philippians 1:29. Why do you think Paul felt that suffering was part of Christ's call on every Christian's life?
2. Read Romans 12:1. What does it mean to present your body as a living sacrifice to God?
3. Think of an example from your life or from the life of someone you know personally that illustrates the suffering versus sacrifice principle in action. Then list some practical ways you can build sacrifice into your life.

11

What's in Your Wallet?

One of my favorite movies is *Vertical Limit*. It's a fictional account of an attempted high-altitude rescue of some stranded climbers on the world's deadliest mountain, K2. Just to show how fictional it is, the rescue climbers strap huge vials of nitroglycerine on their backs and try to make a "speed ascent" up to the dying climbers while at the same time not blowing themselves to smithereens. Such a crazy plan would never be attempted on any real mountain by any real mountaineer, but this is Hollywood. Reality isn't really the point. Like I said, it's one of my favorite movies.

Two of the three rescue parties do end up blowing themselves into oblivion, but the show's star ends up using his vial to rescue most of the climbers, including his younger sister. It was a beautiful moment—I cried. The point of all this is that the rescue parties made the strategic decision to risk everything and to carry an unbelievably dangerous substance on their backs. I contend that we are doing the exact same thing. The substance we carry may not be as volatile, but it's equally dangerous.

Dangerous Stuff

It's money. Be it the plastic or printed kind, that stuff we keep in our wallets and purses can be extremely damaging when not treated carefully. King Solomon, who as we've already seen had a lot of firsthand experience with wealth, asked, "Of what use is money in the hand of a fool, since he has no desire to get wisdom?" (Prov. 17:16). In other words, if we don't have the maturity to handle money wisely, we can actually become enslaved to it. A little later in Proverbs, Solomon commented, "The rich rule over the poor, and the borrower is servant to the lender" (Prov. 22:7). How many of us can identify with being "ruled over" by some financial institution? Overspending, credit, and interest payments have been the demise of more than a few marriages, families, churches, and businesses.

In the New Testament, Paul agrees that money can be very dangerous. One of his statements is perhaps the most misquoted verse in the Bible: "The love of money is a root of all kinds of evil. Some people, eager for money, have wandered from the faith and pierced themselves with many griefs" (1 Tim. 6:10). I'm sure you've heard the misquote: "Money is the root of all evil." But that isn't what Paul said. Money is value neutral; it's neither good nor bad. It's the *love* of money that has caused people to do such evil and irresponsible things throughout history. And we mustn't overlook the second part of what Paul said. When we pursue money, we can stray from the faith and cause ourselves and others much grief. Sound familiar?

So money isn't bad, and having *more than enough* of it isn't necessarily bad either. But it is very much like having a huge canister of nitro strapped to your back—you sure better know what you're doing.

Mirror, Mirror on the Wall

If you want a great indicator of where your values lie, just look at your checkbook. I learned that painful lesson right after Susie and I got married. Susie pays the bills. My job has always been to balance the checkbook at the end of the month. It's a good exercise because it keeps me in touch with where our money is going. So when I first started looking at our books, I couldn't believe how much we were spending on pizza. That's right, pizza! It didn't seem like we ordered in or went out all that often. But when I looked at it on paper, I got a clear picture of just how much we were spending at our local pizza parlor. It wasn't a pretty picture.

Fast-forward to just a few days ago. I was using some tax software to prepare our tax return. I was working on our deductions and I entered the amount that Susie and I had given to our church the previous year. It represented just over 10 percent of our combined gross income. When I entered the amount, the software red-flagged my entry. A little screen popped up saying, "This seems high. Are you sure it's correct?" I love it when that happens. I had my church's year-end giving statement and I could document every penny we'd given. I guess the folks who wrote the software think it's unusual for people to give away over 10 percent of their income. Not to me. It's normal. It's a reflection of what Susie and I value. I just hope my giving still continues to outpace my pizza bill.

What made the change? Actually, Susie and I have always given at least 10 percent of our gross income to our church. We've done so every year of our marriage. But we had to evaluate how we were spending the rest of our money. Thankfully, we figured that having a designated line item for pizza wasn't the best use of our resources, and over the past couple of decades our pizza intake has decreased dramatically.

When Jesus said, "For where your treasure is, there your heart will be also" (Matt. 6:21), he was stating in a timeless fashion the truth I'm trying to explain. It doesn't really matter what we say our priorities are; our money trail shows what we really value. In my world, you'd see that after we pay our tithe our money goes to our mortgage, car payments, college tuition, and then various and sundry other expenses. You'd see that my girls love riding horses and I love backpacking. You'd see that we love the mountains and try to get to Colorado one or two times a year. But most of all, you'd see that a major piece of our time and resources goes to things that are connected to God's kingdom. That's our highest priority, and it should get the best of what we've got.

So here's a little challenge: take a good look at your expenses. It will tell you the truth about who you really are. More specifically, look at where kingdom-related giving stacks up against your other expenses. It's not wrong to spend money on other, less eternally oriented things. In fact, you have to. I just want you to do a fair assessment of where kingdom investment ranks in relation to your other investments. It'll be a good exercise for you—kind of like looking in a mirror or stepping on a scale.

Opportunity Knocks

What's really in your wallet? Potential. The potential to do a world of good for others—to feed the hungry, to house the homeless, and to love and care for orphans. In your wallet is the potential to help bring the message of Jesus to billions of people around the world who have never heard it before. That's right, all that potential is right there in the bottom of your purse or in the pocket of your jeans. I bet you've never thought of your wallet that way, have you?

Look at your short time on earth as one big contest. It's a contest to see who can do the most with what he or she has been given. It's not about how much you get in life, but rather about what you do with what you've been given. Whether it's a lot or a little, it's got potential. What are you doing with it?

I dare you to be different. Anyone can use their resources for their own comfort. That's pretty much standard operating procedure in our culture. And quite frankly, it doesn't take much effort to do so. It's easy to think that what you have in your wallet is not only yours but is there for your benefit. But it takes a different sort of person altogether to see the potential of what he or she has. It takes maturity, an others-centered heart, and a God-centered worldview. Those kind of people look at the world and what's in their wallets in a whole different light. Those kind of people change the world. And those are the folks who are going to have some serious treasures in heaven.

Do you have what it takes to see the potential of your resources? Are you willing to look at your *more than enough* and start releasing it? Because the moment you let it go, the moment you dedicate it to kingdom endeavors, God will start to multiply it. Once you prove to God that you're willing to be a funnel for his resources, he'll just pour it on. He'll give you so much favor, blessing, and kingdom opportunity that you'll have to work not only to keep up with it but to give it away as well.

No Posers Please

My friend Doug Ehrgott works with a missions organization that focuses on Africa. As a result, he spends a lot of time there and meets some very interesting African people. On one of his journeys into a rather remote part of Africa, Doug met a tribal chief who had not yet been exposed to much of our modern culture. On that particular trip, a professional body builder was part of the team that Doug had brought with him. He told me and a few others about a humorous exchange between the chief and the body builder:

> CHIEF: (after staring for a while at the well-developed physique of the body builder) What do you do with all those muscles?
>
> BODY BUILDER: (a little taken aback by the question) What do I do with these muscles?
>
> CHIEF: Yes, what do you do with all those muscles?
>
> BODY BUILDER: Well, I pose.
>
> CHIEF: You pose?
>
> BODY BUILDER: Yes, that's right. I pose.

At this point in his storytelling Doug inserted his own commentary: "That's the American church. We have all this wealth, all these muscles, and yet all we do is pose." Ouch.

After thinking about it, I would narrow Doug's statement a bit: that's the typical American Christian. Most of us have so much wealth, so much muscle, so much kingdom potential, and yet all most of us really do is pose. We look impressive. We clean up nicely and maybe even serve or give some money now and then. But when you look at our potential, when you look at the possible kingdom muscle that God has given us, we're really just playacting. We're posing. And for that we are indeed going to answer to God.

Moving Toward Enough

From Shawn: Your sermon on "Enough" inspired me to reduce our financial overhead, and I started looking for small ways to do so. Here's what I came up with:

1. I stopped using toll roads. Taking the toll road to and from work cuts about 15–20 minutes off of my commute one way. When I stopped taking the toll from work, I ended up saving about $30–$40 a month in toll fees. I also use that 15–20 extra minutes in the car to reflect on my day, meditate, pray, and listen to preaching podcasts.
2. We cut back on Sunday lunch after church. We often eat out Sundays after church because of the convenience. With a family of our size, it's typically around $65. My wife started cooking Crock-Pot meals more often. By the time we get home, it's ready to serve. Doing that twice a month saves us a bit of money as well. She has

also done a lot of research online to cut the cost of our family's average meal.

3. I set aside purposed days of prayer and fasting during lunch.
4. I quit drinking soft drinks during lunch. On average it's $1.25 per drink. That's another $25 a month. Those are just a few small things I have done, but the small sacrifices tend to add up by the end of the month.

For Further Reflection

1. Read 1 Timothy 6:9–10 and list several ways misusing money can be harmful to you.
2. Think about your experience with Christianity and how it might stack up with other expressions of Christianity around the world. Do you agree that we in the Western world are guilty of posing?
3. Read the parable of the talents in Matthew 25:14–30. Which of the three stewards best describes you? Why?

12

Birds and Bees

I remember exactly where I was and what was happening when my parents gave me their respective "birds and bees" talks. My dad gave me his sage advice one night when I was getting ready to go out to a party with some high school buddies. His counsel: "Stay out of the bushes." Actually, that's pretty good advice. Nothing good happens in the bushes, especially at parties.

My mom, on the other hand, took a more strategic approach. She sat on my bedside one night and spilled all the beans. I mean, she gave me the real birds and bees talk. To my horror, and with my older sister giggling from her bedroom next door, she spared no details.

Mom prefaced her talk by saying something like, "Will, I want to tell you something. It's very important. I have to have a talk with you that every parent needs to have with her child. It's time for me to have it with you." Things went downhill from there.

But seriously, I've always been grateful for that talk. My mom told me things I wouldn't have heard otherwise. She told me the truth and cleared up lots of misconceptions for me. And as uncomfortable for me as it may have been, it made me a better man.

So, I want to have a birds and bees talk with you. I want to talk with you about a topic that every Christian needs to know about. It's the best-kept secret in Christianity. It's got the potential to radically change your life for the better. And, more importantly, it's something God requires of you.

I'm talking, of course, about giving. Let's pretend we're meeting over coffee at a local café. Let me share some important information with you and even answer the questions that I get asked most frequently. I promise to give you short, honest, biblical answers. My guess is that like the other birds and bees talk, this one will make you uncomfortable initially. But stay with me. You'll be glad you did.

Do You Know Your GPR?

Something that I've never seen in any church, anywhere, is for the preacher to tell the congregation to stop giving. No way. But it really happened once. Too much money had been collected, so the pastor stood up and actually commanded the people to stop giving. Seriously? That's enough to get you defrocked in some denominations.

The "pastor" was Moses, and the people were the Israelites. Here's the account:

Then Moses summoned Bezalel and Oholiab and every skilled person to whom the LORD had given ability and who was willing to come and do the work. They received from Moses all the offerings the Israelites had brought to carry out the work of constructing the sanctuary. And the people continued to bring freewill offerings morning after morning. So all the skilled craftsmen who were doing all the work on the sanctuary left their work and said to Moses, "The people are bringing more than enough for doing the work the LORD commanded to be done." Then Moses gave an order and they sent this word throughout the camp: "No man or woman is to make anything else as an offering for the sanctuary." And so the people were restrained from bringing more, because what they already had was more than enough to do all the work. (Exod. 36:2–7)

Did you happen to catch those words in the last sentence? ". . . because what they already had was *more than enough* to do all the work." Hmm. . . .

Why did the people give so much? Why did Moses have to command them to stop giving? I believe it was because of their GPR factor.

The *G* in GPR is for *gratitude*. I know the Israelites had their bad moments, but they still remembered what it was like to be slaves in Egypt. As bad as things were for them, they were still far better off than they had been under Pharaoh's wrath. They were still grateful for God's deliverance, and gratitude always drives generosity.

The *P* stands for *perspective*. The Israelites who gave so generously of their stuff knew, actually, that it wasn't their stuff. They remembered God's command for them to plunder the Egyptians on their way out of Egypt. God had planned for this all along. During his encounter with Moses at the burning bush, God had said, "I will make the Egyptians favorably disposed toward this people, so that when you leave you will not go empty-handed. Every woman is to ask her neighbor and any woman living in her house for articles of silver and gold and for clothing, which you will put on your sons and daughters. And so you will plunder the Egyptians" (Exod. 3:21–22). And on that terrible night when the death angel had passed through Egypt, while the Egyptians were grieving their dead, "The Israelites did as Moses instructed and asked the Egyptians for articles of silver and gold and for clothing. The Lord had made the Egyptians favorably disposed toward the people, and they gave them what they asked for; so they plundered the Egyptians" (Exod. 12:35–36). Talk about an awkward conversation: "Hey, I'm really sorry about your son. And by the way, can I have that vase?"

There was no way the Israelites could forget how God had provided for them. They'd left Egypt with a load of loot specifically provided as materials for the tabernacle that God would command them to build. They knew what they had, who had given it to them, and what it was for. That's perspective. And when you have that kind of perspective, giving becomes second nature.

The *R* in GPR is for *reverence,* which is a nicely dressed word for *fear.* To fear God is to revere him, to be in awe of him. It doesn't mean to really be scared of him, but rather to have a healthy respect for him. Fear, respect, honor, and reverence all drive giving.

The Israelites knew enough about God to know that they shouldn't mismanage the resources he'd given them. They'd seen the ten plagues, the Red Sea crossing, and even the ground opening up and swallowing the bad guys—enough to know that you didn't mess with God or his property. So when it came time to give they did so out of a healthy respect for God.

Such respect is missing in many Christian circles these days. Those of us with *more than enough* rarely think about why we have it. We're just glad we do and we do all we can to enjoy it. Most of us never stop to wonder why God has so blessed us, and that may well be a reflection of our lack of reverence for him and his gifts.

SOP

Giving is supposed to be SOP—standard operating procedure—for Christ-followers. Not giving, or more specifically, not giving a minimum of 10 percent to your church, isn't a biblical option. And yet for many American Christians, *not* giving has become the standard. It's an embarrassing statistic, but well less than 10 percent of American Christians say they actually tithe.[1] And as the pastor of a rather affluent church, I know firsthand that only about 20 percent of our church members tithe.

But such financial stinginess isn't the biblical norm. Even though tithing is an Old Testament concept, the themes of generous and sacrificial giving run from cover to cover in the Bible.

God expects every Christ-follower to excel in the spiritual discipline of giving. Here's just a small sampling:

- "A tithe of everything from the land, whether grain from the soil or fruit from the trees, belongs to the LORD; it is holy to the LORD" (Lev. 27:30).
- "As soon as the order went out, the Israelites generously gave the firstfruits of their grain, new wine, oil and

honey and all that the fields produced. They brought a great amount, a tithe of everything" (2 Chron. 31:5).

- "One man gives freely, yet gains even more; another withholds unduly, but comes to poverty. A generous man will prosper; he who refreshes others will himself be refreshed" (Prov. 11:24–25).

- "'Bring the whole tithe into the storehouse, that there may be food in my house. Test me in this,' says the LORD Almighty, 'and see if I will not throw open the floodgates of heaven and pour out so much blessing that you will not have room enough for it'" (Mal. 3:10).

- "But just as you excel in everything—in faith, in speech, in knowledge, in complete earnestness and in your love for us—see that you also excel in this grace of giving" (2 Cor. 8:7).

- "Remember this: Whoever sows sparingly will also reap sparingly, and whoever sows generously will also reap generously. Each man should give what he has decided in his heart to give, not reluctantly or under compulsion, for God loves a cheerful giver" (2 Cor. 9:6–7).

What's the point? Giving is normal. It's what Christians do.

Motive Matters

Maybe you've wondered, "Why should I give? Why do preachers make such a big deal about it? It's hard not to think that all they want is money so they can build bigger churches. Can you give me even one solid reason that I should part with at least 10 percent of my hard-earned money?" Sure. Here are several great reasons to become a regular, generous giver:

1. *God modeled giving.* The best-known verse in the Bible reads, "For God so loved the world that he gave . . ." (John 3:16). God set the standard of giving for his people. He set it at a level that we ourselves can never reach, because he gave his Son for us. But since God is our Father, his example of radical giving also sets the expectation for us. If he gave radically, how can we do any less?

2. *God honors giving.* Any consistent giver will tell you that they will never quit giving. Once you've experienced the favor and blessing that God shows to your financial obedience, you'll never want it to stop. God always honors obedience, and he always honors the obedience of giving. Susie and I have given 10 percent or more of our income every month of our marriage (we were married in June of 1985). We have seen God honor our obedience in astounding ways. I'm not saying that God makes us financially rich; far from it. Giving isn't a spiritual get-rich-quick scheme. But we both know that God has done far more with the 85 to 90 percent of the money left after we give than we could ever have done with the full 100 percent. God is much better at stretching and managing our resources (really his resources) than we are. We're still not sure how it all works out, but we know God honors our giving. He will honor yours too.

3. *Giving honors God.* Giving is an act of worship. In the centuries before Christ, when an Israelite offered a lamb, a pigeon, or some type of grain offering to God, it was an act of worship. It was seen as a gift to God. When you write a check, give stock, or make a

cash gift of some kind to your church, it is also an act of worship. The point of giving is that God deserves our best. To offer our tithes to God is to declare that we'd rather honor him with our best than receive any potential benefit it might bring us. It declares that he is the highest priority of our lives. Giving is simply one of the purest and most direct ways we can honor and worship God.

4. *Giving is a declaration of dependence.* When you give your best and first to God, you're stating that your hope and faith are in him, not in your resources. Giving acknowledges that God is the giver of all gifts and that our eyes are on him for our daily provision. If you find that you're getting too dependent on your salary, your investments, your insurance, or your retirement fund for your security and provision, then you probably aren't writing big enough checks to your church. Giving is a great way to confess that God is a source of your *more than enough* and that you intend to use it well and not hoard or misuse it.

Nuts and Bolts

How much should I give? The Old Testament minimum was 10 percent. God's people were expected to give a tenth of their produce or profits as sacrifices and gifts to God. Beyond that, many special offerings were required throughout the year. The typical Jew would have known nothing of a life that didn't include consistent giving.

And that was before the new covenant—before grace was made available to us; before the outpouring of God's Spirit;

and most importantly, before Jesus gave his life for us. So here's another million-dollar question: If God's people, who were only under the Law and who knew nothing of the intimacy of God's Spirit and the sacrifice of Jesus' blood, gave at least a tenth of all they had to God, can we really do any less? Should we be comfortable giving less than what they did? The least we can do is honor God's Old Testament command to give 10 percent. In reality, we should all do better, much better.

Gross or net? I actually had a guy ask me over lunch one time if he could give only based on his net earnings. I almost came across the table at him. Seriously? The answer is gross. Give to God before the government and your IRA take their shares. In fact, give as much as you can. God will honor it in amazing ways. Remember, it's all his anyway.

How often should I give? I believe there is some wiggle room on this one, as in today's world people get paid differently. I get paid every two weeks, so we give on those paychecks. Some people get paid monthly; others don't see any real income until the end of the year. So here's a good rule of thumb: give as often as you have increase. If you receive weekly, then give weekly. If you receive monthly, then give monthly.

The point of giving is to respond to the Lord's increase in your life. So whenever and however he chooses to give you increase, give on that.

Where should I give? Can I spread my tithe around, or do I have to give it all in one place? I encourage Christians to give their first tenth to the place where they "hang their hat" spiritually. I think this may be what the Lord meant when he said, "Bring your whole tithe to the storehouse" (Mal. 3:10).

From the New Testament standpoint, I believe that the part of Christ's body in which you live, serve, and worship needs to receive your first tenth. If you and/or your family are being discipled there, then you need to give your first tenth there. Beyond that, I think you should give to as many Christian causes and ministries as you feel led to. Remember, in regard to giving it's never an either-or proposition. The answer, instead, is always yes.

Let me explain. I recently met with a member of our church who was planning to reduce his giving by $10,000 so that he could have his employer match his gift to a nonprofit our church supports. The business wouldn't give directly to the church, but they would give to the other ministry. The man felt that it wasn't right to "leave $10,000 on the table" and he redirected 10K of his gifts to the other ministry so that his employer would match it. To his credit, he wrote and told us of his intentions. And then, even more to his credit, he agreed to meet with me to talk about it.

I encouraged him to keep giving his tithe to our church. And then I encouraged him to make the $10,000 gift to the nonprofit. God was obviously leading him to serve this other ministry, something we wanted to encourage. But I didn't believe God was leading him to decrease his support of his home base of ministry to do it. So I told him, "The answer is yes, not either-or." He grinned and replied, "Somehow I knew you were going to say that."

Always start by giving your tenth to the place you call home spiritually. Make sure your church gets your first and best. After that, have at it. God will honor your generosity.

What happens if I don't give? Nothing—literally. You won't receive the blessing and favor that God promised to those who give: "Honor the LORD with your wealth, with the firstfruits of all your crops; then your barns will be filled to overflowing, and your vats will brim over with new wine" (Prov. 3:9–10).

God honors giving. If you choose to not give, then you're settling for your best, not his.

But something else happens if you don't give—needs go unmet. There really are consequences to disobedience, and those consequences always have ripple effects. God has given you *more than enough* so that you can serve and encourage those with *less than enough*. Neighbors, loved ones, and friends may have specific needs that you can meet. Ministries and missions across town and around the world can use what God has given you to help the needy. If you don't release it, those needs go unmet. And given that most churches and ministries are on the front lines of serving the poor, the at-risk, the spiritual and physical captives, those unmet needs have major implications.

In August of 2005, Hurricane Katrina slammed into the Gulf Coast. It was one of the deadliest and certainly most costly natural disasters in US history. As I write this, it's been nearly six years since the storm. But hundreds of ministries and churches (including ours) are still sending money, resources, and people to serve the Gulf Coast area. More than one pastor in the area has told me that if the church hadn't come to the aid of those suffering, nothing would have gotten done. The government simply wasn't ready to respond to a crisis of such magnitude. But the church was.

Within hours of the storm's passing, dozens and dozens of relief teams from churches all over the country descended on the area. What occurred in the months that followed was one of the largest relief and restoration efforts in our nation's history, and it's still going on today. And it was entirely volunteer driven, privately funded, and below the government's and media's radar. Those with *more than enough* came to the aid of those who suddenly found themselves with *less than enough* and the rest, quite literally, is history.

But what kind of shape would the Gulf Coast be in today if the church hadn't responded? Think of the needs that would have gone unmet and the lives that would have been trapped in despair and suffering if people hadn't given sacrificially on their behalf. That's what happens when you don't give—needs don't get met.

You Can't Out-Give God

[Written and submitted by Andrea and Jason Thomas. Andrea and Jason are on staff with InterVarsity Christian Fellowship on the University of Texas campus. You can read more of Andrea's writings at ispygod.com.]

Andrea: My Grandma and Grandpa Meyer had a remarkable marriage. They adored each other and were together over sixty years before Grandpa passed away in November of 2000. In the spring of 2006, my grandmother joined Grandpa, succumbing to breast cancer that had metastasized in her brain.

My grandparents left an inheritance to each of their three sons, and my parents gave Jason and me $10,000 from it. About the same time as we received this inheritance, we read a wonderful little book called *The Treasure Principle* by Randy Alcorn (see http://www.epm.org). In it, Randy challenges his readers not to hold on to earthly wealth but to invest it for eternity. So we were faced with a decision about what to do with this unexpected money, and we felt convicted that we weren't giving enough to serve the poor.

Of course, there were plenty of reasons to keep the inheritance, the most pressing being our need for a new minivan. With over 120,000 miles, the Chevy Venture was having lots of problems and we knew it wasn't going to last. For several years we'd been saving up to buy a newer vehicle, and we had our eyes on a used Honda Odyssey. The inheritance would ensure that we could afford a later-model Odyssey. Or we could put the money in funds for our kids' college educations.

For me, giving away the inheritance meant saying "no" to lots of little things I wanted. To Jason it meant letting go of the security of an emergency fund. You can probably guess which of us has the gift of spending and which has the gift of saving.

Jason: We initially decided to tithe 10 percent of the inheritance and to put the rest in a CD as a needed emergency reserve fund for our family. After several weeks, we began to feel a burden and desire to use all this "unearned" money to serve the poor. Our initial plan was to give it away slowly to missions over time. But in December, Andrea felt led to give it all away. After my initial resistance, I agreed, and we donated the remaining $9,000 to the poor at Urbana, Inter-Varsity's mission convention.

Andrea: Jason attended Urbana on our behalf and gave the gift as part of an offering that raised more than a million dollars for the poor around the world. For both of us, giving that inheritance was a wonderfully freeing act of obedience that brought great joy.

And then the storm hit. That same December, a tumor began to grow in my right breast. Thinking it was just another cyst, I didn't give it much attention. But by April I had been diagnosed with an aggressive stage II breast cancer. I was only 35. Our three children were eight, six, and two at the time. The diagnosis launched us into a world of decisions and crisis. While it was a tragedy to see my grandmother die of breast cancer in her eighties, it was another to personally face the statistic that even after undergoing a mastectomy, I had a 50/50 chance of surviving to celebrate my forty-sixth birthday. But by undergoing chemotherapy and Tamoxifen treatments, I would increase my ten-year survival rate to 85 percent.

At about the same time, two of our key staff directors in Dallas and Houston left. Both left for good reasons and we blessed them, but the timing was tough and their departure meant much more work for Jason as I would be on medical leave. Additionally, May and June are key months to do year-end fund-raising for our ministry. We were facing a large deficit with almost no time to work to erase it. We hadn't had a pay raise in two years and were starting to feel the stress of upcoming medical bills. All we could do was pray.

Jason: Not long after that, I went to our mailbox, returned to my car, and opened up an envelope addressed to us from our church. In it was a check for $10,000, the exact amount we'd chosen to give away. I was absolutely dumbfounded by our church's generosity during our time of crisis. After getting over the shock and tears, I broke out in songs of praise to Jesus. (Thankfully, only my two-year-old son Josiah was in the car!)

Andrea: Yes, our church gave us $10,000, knowing nothing about the inheritance we'd given away! And the story doesn't stop there. We've received many more unsolicited gifts from the generosity of friends, family, and even strangers—house cleaning every other week, numerous meals, weekly laundry service,

$2,500 to help cover medical bills, and lots of cards and smaller tokens of love. I got some new clothes and a few new hairstyles, as my mom and dear friend Margaret bought me wigs.

Remember that minivan need? Again, completely unsolicited and with no idea about the inheritance we gave away, Jason's parents decided to give us their 2003 Honda Odyssey, worth probably $20,000! In the end, we received back four times the $10,000, as well as just about everything else we thought we were giving away!

The Lord brought us through the storms at home and work, all the while blessing us in the process. My cancer is gone, my treatments are finished, Jason effectively did the work of three people for a season, the ministry at the University of Texas continues to grow, our children seem to be flourishing, and we have basked in a season of receiving love, prayers, and gifts from friends and family around the world.

Moving Toward Enough

From Rebekah, age seventeen: Right now I'm making bracelets. At first I just thought I'd make about twenty or twenty-five to give to the kids in Nicaragua the next time I go. I went out to Michael's and bought a ton of string and a little kit. (Side note: I have a missions fund. It's for raising money to help me and my family go on missions trips to Nicaragua, and for buying things for the kids down there.) So I figured making all these bracelets would get boring fast. I asked God to give me the desire and passion to continue to make them. I've made about ten today! I also asked him for guidance with whatever else he wants done with this project. This morning I was talking to my mom. We came up with the idea of selling them at soccer tournaments for the suggested donation of $5. All of the proceeds will go to the missions fund. My parents and brothers even bought one!

For Further Reflection

1. Why do you think money management and giving are such tough subjects to talk about? Why do so many people resent sermons about giving? How could the local church do a better job of teaching money management and giving without appearing to be money hungry?
2. Are you a giver? Be honest with yourself. How much of your annual income do you actually give away? How do you determine how much you give and where it goes? If you're a tither, can you relate to the principle, "God honors giving"?
3. What is your response to Andrea and Jason's story? Do you think they should have given their inheritance to a missions cause? Would you have done that? What do you think is the point of their story?

13

How to Be an Upper Room Christian

Then came the day of Unleavened Bread on which the Passover lamb had to be sacrificed. Jesus sent Peter and John, saying, "Go and make preparations for us to eat the Passover."

"Where do you want us to prepare for it?" they asked.

He replied, "As you enter the city, a man carrying a jar of water will meet you. Follow him to the house that he enters, and say to the owner of the house, 'The Teacher asks: Where is the guest room, where I may eat the Passover with my disciples?' He will show you a large upper room, all furnished. Make preparations there."

They left and found things just as Jesus had told them. So they prepared the Passover.

Luke 22:7–13

Who Was That Masked Man?

He's one of the most significant figures in the New Testament, and yet he's unnamed. In fact, we know very little about him at all. I'm talking about the man vaguely mentioned in the passage above, the owner of the upper room.

If you think about it, the upper room may be one of the most important rooms or buildings mentioned in the Bible. In that room, Jesus celebrated his final Passover with his disciples and then translated the beautiful celebration into Holy Communion. It was in the upper room that Jesus washed his disciples' feet and dismissed Judas to his evil task. It appears that the upper room was where several of the disciples stayed in the days after the resurrection of Jesus, and Jesus appeared to them there on at least two different occasions. And the upper room is where the 120 disciples waited in prayer for ten days before God unleashed his Spirit on them and the New Testament church was born. That's quite a legacy for one room!

The owner of that room proved to be quite a visionary. He took a risk on Jesus and his disciples when others might have thought it too dangerous to do so. He opened his home to them without knowing how their story would end. He was also gracious and hospitable enough to house and feed a large group of people for several weeks after Jesus' resurrection. The owner of the upper room wanted to use his resources to serve Christ, even if he wasn't fully sure what "serving Christ" meant. He had a room—a large one—and he felt like it shouldn't be wasted. And it's his attitude that I pray I'll have more of.

Putting Your Upper Room Where Your Heart Is

There comes a point in the life of every believer, and specifically for those who live with *more than enough*, when they feel

188

led to start using what God has given them. Several wealthy or educated or strategically placed followers of Jesus made similar sacrifices. Consider Mary, Martha, and Lazarus. The three siblings owned a large house and winepress in the small village of Bethany, not far from Jerusalem. Their estate became a popular resting place for Jesus and his disciples. Their home became the site of one of Jesus' best-known miracles, the raising of Lazarus.

Also consider Joseph of Arimathea, who risked his political future as a member of the Sanhedrin by offering his very expensive tomb in Jerusalem for Jesus' burial. At some point Joseph had come to believe that Jesus was the Christ. After the crucifixion, he saw an opportunity to serve Jesus and his disciples by offering his own tomb. His upper room act of kindness must have been a relief and comfort to Jesus' grieving disciples.

Or what about Mary, the mother of John Mark, mentioned in Acts 12? Her home became the site of an all-night prayer vigil for Peter after Herod had arrested him. The house was large enough to hold the dozens of people who turned out to intercede for Peter's rescue. It must have been well known to the disciples because it was the first place Peter went when he realized he was free.

Then there's Lydia, the wealthy seller of purple dye, who became the first convert in Philippi. She opened her home to Paul and his traveling companions and it ended up becoming the first meeting place of the church in Philippi.

And we mustn't forget Paul, the wealthy, sophisticated, educated expert in the law of Moses. This unlikely disciple leveraged his education and position to become history's greatest defender of the Christian faith.

We could continue this survey right through history to the present day. Your faith, your position, and your resources—they're all things you can leverage for God's kingdom work. And when you do, when you simply release what God has given you for his purposes, then like the owner of the upper room, like Joseph, Lydia, and countless others, God can use it to do far more than you ever imagined.

We Don't Have an Upper Room, but We Can Help Pay for One

In 1993, Susie and I felt God leading us to start a church in our hometown of Austin. We were full of vision and passion for our city, but that's about all we had. We had no resources to put toward such an endeavor. I mean zippo, nada. If we were going to start a church in Austin, either I was going to have to work bi-vocationally and Susie would also have to work, or someone was going to have to underwrite us. We started praying for the latter and preparing for the former.

Enter two friends whom I'll simply call Blake and Connie. I knew this couple because their son and I were close friends in college. They had visited my church occasionally and had tried to keep up with me when I moved to Fort Worth to continue my education. One day, a few months after Susie and I had started praying about returning to Austin, and long before we had told anybody what we were thinking, Blake called out of the blue. He said he wanted to get together and catch up.

At the time, I was too young and naïve to know that men like Blake rarely set a meeting just because they want to catch up. God, Blake, and Connie were up to something; I just didn't know it. They were two upper room Christians ready to put their assets to work for their Savior.

Susie and I sat down with Connie and Blake a few weeks later. I don't remember exactly how the conversation went, but they said something like this: "We believe in you two. We think you need to be in Austin. If you'd be willing to come back to Austin and start a church, we'd be willing to fund it . . . at least for a while." God had answered our prayers; we had our underwriter.

It would be difficult to measure the impact of Blake and Connie's investments in the kingdom. Since we started Austin Christian Fellowship (ACF) in 1994, I have seen countless examples of lives being changed and people turning to Christ—all as a result of their upper room mind-set. To say that God has used ACF would be a massive understatement, and it all started when Blake and Connie were obedient to a nudge.

Looking back, I see how God had woven our lives together. Blake and I had an unlikely friendship—we ran in completely different worlds and were in totally different seasons of life. But God put us together. He knew we'd need each other. I believe God raised up Blake and Connie to help ACF get off the ground. We couldn't have done it without them. And I believe God raised up Susie and me to show Connie and Blake how much joy they could find in funding kingdom work.

What has God raised you up for? Why has he given you *more than enough*? Were you to redirect some of your resources—your time, your money, your talents—what could you do? You may not have the resources to fund someone's ministry for a year, but you do have *more than enough* for a reason. Someone is out there praying right now for a miraculous provision from God. Maybe you're their answer.

You Too Can Be an Upper Room Christian

Upper room Christianity isn't just for those who have a large house or significant financial resources. Anyone can be an upper room Christian. Take a look at what you have, at where you work, at your education, at your gifts and talents. What needs around you do you suddenly seem perfectly suited to meet?

- You've got a used car you want to trade in, and the single mom across the street just happens to need a car.
- You're a dentist, and your church just happens to be launching a medical missions effort in a third world country.
- You're a retired empty nester, and the family down the street just happens to need some help watching their kids.
- You're great with numbers and bookkeeping, and a nonprofit in town just happens to need some accounting help.
- You're a skilled musician, and a school in your neighborhood just happens to need a volunteer to work with their musically gifted kids.
- You and your spouse have a good income and two extra bedrooms, and there just happens to be a waiting list for foster kids to be placed in safe homes.
- Your church has a budget deficit, and the amount they need just happens to be the same as the amount you've been thinking about investing.

- You work in a county detention facility, and a well-known criminal just happens to be placed under your watch.
- A friend is struggling with a drinking problem, and you just happen to have fifteen years of sobriety.
- A co-worker just buried his father and is asking questions about life and death, and you just happen to be a Christian.

That's how upper room Christians get started. They see a need and then realize that they are perfectly set up to meet it. It may look like a coincidence, but try telling that to the owner of the upper room.

Moving Toward Enough

From Jimmy and Jeannie: Our journey toward enough started with a simple decision. We decided to sit out one entire season of sports with our kids. With three kids in three different sports leagues, it seemed as if we were always driving from one practice or game to another. But after we went cold turkey on sports, suddenly we had all this extra time to just be together. We talked more, ate together more, watched movies together, slept late, and most of all, we got to know our kids better. Beyond that, our intimacy with each other and the Lord increased dramatically, and we knew there was more of both if we were willing to pursue them. That led us to start thinking how we could further simplify our lives. It's strange, but we didn't know how much sports and busyness controlled us until we walked away from them. But we're glad we did. Today we know our kids, each other, and most of all, God, better.

For Further Reflection

1. In your own words, define "upper room Christianity." What are the attributes that upper room Christians seem to have in common?
2. Has your life been impacted by the giving of an upper room Christian? Who was that person, and what did he or she do that impacted you?
3. What is your upper room? What resources, experience, education, and skills do you have that God might use to benefit others?

Less Is More

*He must become greater;
I must become less.*

John the Baptist, as
quoted in John 3:30

14

"Less" Thinking

Recently, while on one of my trips to Nicaragua, I realized on my last day there that I still had several hundred cordobas left in my wallet. The cordoba is the Nicaraguan currency, but it's worth a lot less than the American dollar. The average exchange rate is thirty or forty cordobas to one dollar. I had well over a hundred cords left and I knew that they would do me no good back in the States. But a hundred cords in Nicaragua is a lot of money—twice as much as a typical worker might make in a day.

And then I had a revelation: I was rich and I needed to give it all away! I can't tell you how much fun I had that last day in Managua. I left huge tips for the waitress at lunch and overpaid for everything I purchased. I was giving away money like it was going out of style. And with every act of supposed generosity on my part came the smiles, gasps, and even tears on the part of the recipients. That was the most fun I'd had in a long time. I loved thinking I was rich (even if it was for a day) and being so generous.

The next day, while on the flight home, the Holy Spirit started talking to me. He said something like this:

Will, you really enjoyed yesterday, didn't you? You loved being so generous and free with your money. I was proud of you. You encouraged a lot of people. But guess what? You're still rich! You can still be just as generous and giving as you were yesterday! You see, where you are going your money is worthless. The American dollar is no more valuable in heaven than the cordoba is in the United States. So you don't need to keep your dollars. They're not going to do you any good. I'll take care of your needs while you're on earth. I'll help you with college and medical expenses and even retirement, if it ever comes for you. But I want you to keep on living like you're rich, because you are. Keep on sharing your money and resources. Be overly generous with them. When I give you blessings, financial or otherwise, I don't want you to keep them. Pass them around. Let's see how much fun we can have and how many people we can bless before you get to heaven.

Needless to say, that was a profound day for me. I'd never really seen myself as rich before, but compared to the world's standards I'm fabulously wealthy. And beyond that, besides earthly wealth, I am infinitely rich. As one of God's children I have access to the unlimited resources of my heavenly Father. He has already taken care of all my needs. So while I have earthly wealth, I need to share it with those who don't.

You know what? If you're a Christian, you're fabulously rich too. So why not start giving away what you have. Try thinking "less": give away as much as you can and live on as little as you can. You're really not going to need it.

Five Practices of "Less" Thinkers

People who are moving toward *enough*, people who have learned to look at their lives and resources through the "less is more" filter, usually practice several disciplines to help keep their thinking set on less. Here are five of those common disciplines.

- *Regular reality checks.* People with a "less is more" mind-set stay in touch with reality. It's easy to get enamored with wealth and comfortable living and to start thinking that such things really matter. They don't. In fact, they're not even real. The apostle Paul reminded us of this truth when he wrote, "Therefore we do not lose heart. Though outwardly we are wasting away, yet inwardly we are being renewed day by day. For our light and momentary troubles are achieving for us an eternal glory that far outweighs them all. So we fix our eyes not on what is seen, but on what is unseen. For what is seen is temporary, but what is unseen is eternal" (2 Cor. 4:16–18). If you can see it, touch it, and own it, then ultimately it's not real. It's going to perish and give way to that which is real, the eternal and the invisible. To think "less" you've got to learn to think invisible, intangible, and eternal. Don't fall prey to the lie that what we experience in this life is all there is. It isn't.

- *Looking ahead.* Hand in hand with knowing what's real is the discipline of looking ahead. Moses was lauded for his forward thinking by the writer of Hebrews: "By faith Moses, when he had grown up, refused to be known as the son of Pharaoh's daughter. He chose to be mistreated along with the people of God rather than to enjoy the pleasures of sin for a short time. He regarded disgrace for the sake of Christ as of greater value than the treasures of Egypt, because he was looking ahead to his reward" (Heb. 11:24–26). Moses could have easily chosen to grasp the power and wealth that were his in Egypt. But he chose not to. He shared in the suffering of his people by sacrificing what many would have said was rightfully his. He looked ahead, and in doing so gained an eternal reward. As we move toward *enough*, we'll want to learn to do the same.

- *Sabbath.* I know that Sabbath really shouldn't be a new or novel concept, but the reality is that many of us have no real Sabbath rest in our lives, or even really know what Sabbath means. But practicing Sabbath is a critical part of moving toward *enough* and developing a "less is more" mind-set. Sabbath is the discipline of slowing down—actually, that's wrong. It's the discipline of stopping. Working seven days a week and not stopping for Sabbath only erodes your contentment and leads you back into the never-ending, unsatisfying pursuit of more. When you practice Sabbath, you take a twenty-four-hour break from anything that could benefit you, cause you to "get ahead," or make you money in any way. In modern language, it's shutting down email, not checking stock futures, postponing work-related calls, and pretty much fasting from anything that isn't directly connected to loving God or loving the people he has placed into your life. "Less" thinkers know the value of gearing back for a full twenty-four hours to pursue God and reset their priorities and perspectives to what really matters.

- *Contentment.* The tenth commandment instructs us not to covet what our neighbors have. Stated positively, we're to develop a contented heart. That can be a real challenge when those around me appear to be enjoying their nicer cars, better clothes, and bigger houses. If I'm not careful, I can become jealous of what they have and discontented with what God has graciously given me. So I'm learning to celebrate what others achieve and acquire. When a friend, co-worker, or neighbor gets a new car, a promotion, or something else, I discipline myself to celebrate with and for them. If God has chosen to honor them in such a fashion, who am I to rain on their parade with my sorry attitude. Practice rejoicing in the favor God shows to others. It will make you more content with what he has done for you.

- *Gratitude.* Those who have learned to think "less" are great at openly and regularly thanking God for his provision, even in the little details of their lives. My wife Susie keeps a gratitude journal. She's disciplined herself to frequently write down how God has blessed her lately. In doing so, she is cultivating a grateful spirit in herself that quickly spills over into our family. Gratitude is contagious, and it's a powerful discipline in the battle to become a "less is more" thinker. Remember what Paul told the believers in Thessalonica: "Be joyful always; pray continually; give thanks in all circumstances, for this is God's will for you in Christ Jesus" (1 Thess. 5:16–18).

Just Keep It

In the early days of Austin Christian Fellowship, way back in the mid-1990s, we were a start-up organization in every sense. We were always financially strapped and didn't even buy pencils without praying about it. So when we decided to add our first new staff member, we moved very slowly and prayed like crazy. Actually, we prayed for a sign. We asked God to show us in an undeniable way whether or not we could afford to make the hire.

Just a few days later the sign came. We got a call from a stockbroker telling us that he had been instructed by a client to sell $15,000 of a certain stock and give it to ACF. We went bonkers! The 15K was almost half of what we planned to pay the new staffer. We figured that God had spoken and that we had our sign. Within a few days the new staff member joined us in our small offices and went to work. We were thrilled. God had come through.

And then the phone call came. The next week we got a call from the same stockbroker. He apologized and said that he had made a terrible mistake. As he was reviewing his records, he discovered that the sell order for his client had been for $1,500, not $15,000. Uh, oops. We were now looking at a "sign" that was significantly smaller than what we thought. The really funny part of this is that the new staff member took the call. I'll never forget when he walked into my office to give me the news. He was white as a sheet and looked like he might get sick right then and there. After helping him to a chair, I got on the phone and called the man who had donated the stock. I had already contacted him once to thank him, but we had not discussed the specific amount of his gift. This time I told him what the broker had said—that he had made a $13,500 mistake! The man sounded embarrassed and a little confused and asked if he could call me back. He did within the hour.

What he said then goes down in our church's history as one of the coolest moments we can all remember. He simply said, "Just keep it." Then he added, "I didn't even know I had $15,000 of that stock. Obviously God wanted me to give it to you, so just keep it."

After I hung up, we sang, laughed, cried, and did the happy dance. And then I commented how I would have loved to hear the conversation between the man and his stockbroker.

The loose manner in which that giver held his resources represents the kind of "less is more" thinking that people have who are moving toward *enough*. He saw a kingdom need and moved to meet it. When a mistake happened that caused him to give much more than he intended, he didn't even think twice. He figured God had big plans for us and for that money. He figured it was God's money anyway and that God could do with it as he pleased. I've talked with that man several times since his decision to let us keep the money; he's never once regretted it.

Moving Toward Enough

From Anna: I started practicing "less is more" living eleven years ago. That was about the time I quit my job as an actuary to stay at home after our son was born. There are so many things I have learned to do to save money over the years. We drive much older cars (we have been without car payments for four years); I shop for clothes at discount stores; I get hand-me-downs from my sisters or other friends; and I take furniture that other people want to get rid of. We are not too proud to do these things! My husband and I have made a commitment to really stick to our budget this year and become debt free. We are giving up a lot this year and the kids are on board. For example, this past week for spring break our vacation was a day trip to a local state park. It only cost us gas money and $12 to get in! And you know what? We had a blast! The kids didn't need an expensive trip skiing or to the beach. They just wanted to be with us!

I want to say that the reason we are so blessed and have a very different perspective on monetary things is because of our faith in Christ. It can be easy to get swept away with all the "stuff" out there and the lies that we hear every day about buying more. I really feel sorry for the people who try to fill the holes of their lives with material possessions. I am so happy with my husband, my life, and the choices we have made to live with less to have such a more fulfilling life!

For Further Reflection

1. Read and meditate on Psalm 37:25–26. Think about how you can be like the "righteous" these verses describe.
2. Why does pursuing less instead of more seem so counter-intuitive? List some of the pressures we all feel to always have more.
3. Of the five practices of "less" thinkers listed above, which one do you think you most need to build into your life? Why?

15

"Less" Potential

In the uniqueness of God's economy, the less you have, the more you have. The more you release, the more you get. And the little you do have, when given to God, gains infinite potential.

What Do You Have in Your Hand?

God isn't in the habit of asking questions of others. I mean, it's not like he's lacking information. So when he does ask questions, it's typically because he wants to get someone to think about something. Such was the case when he questioned Moses in their conversation at the burning bush (see Exodus 3 and 4). Some of the questions God put to Moses were merely rhetorical, but the first question God asked Moses was designed to get him thinking: "Moses, what do you have in your hand?"

It was a simple question really. Moses might even have been a little taken aback by it. God obviously knew what Moses had in his hand. It was his shepherd's staff. It would have been no more than three or four inches in diameter and anywhere from five to seven feet long. Shepherds used staffs to herd and even correct wayward sheep and to fight off anything that might threaten them or their flocks. Beyond that, the staff wasn't much more than a big, long stick. And it was probably all Moses had with him at the time. Whatever Moses' resources were at the point of his calling, he certainly didn't have anything near what it would cost to travel back to Egypt, mount a successful assault against Pharaoh's armies, and then lead his starving nation to the Promised Land. No, all Moses had was a simple shepherd's staff, and that was next to nothing.

But that was all he needed, and that was God's point. You see, when it comes to doing God's work, we don't want the best we can do. If we try to do God's work by relying on our best, then that's all we're going to get—*our* best. But if we rely on God's provision and power rather than our own, then we'll get *his* best. And it's when we get God's best that lives get changed and entire nations are set free.

Nothing Matters

As long as we have wealth, resources, connections, and earthly power at our disposal, we'll be tempted to rely on those things instead of God. That's why God often strips us down to almost nothing—to having a mere shepherd's staff—before he uses us. When we're empty-handed we have nothing to rely on but his power. And that's when he does his best work through us.

- That's why God used an obscure, insignificant people to reveal his plan and love to the world.
- That's why God chose a ruddy teenager, a stone, and a sling to kill a mighty giant.
- That's why God used a small army of three hundred to defeat an army of thousands.
- That's why God chose an unknown Hebrew girl to be the mother of his Son.
- That's why Jesus chose relatively uneducated fishermen to be his disciples.

That's why Paul told the Corinthian believers that "God chose the foolish things of the world to shame the wise; God chose the weak things of the world to shame the strong. He chose the lowly things of this world and the despised things—and the things that are not—to nullify the things that are, so that no one may boast before him" (1 Cor. 1:27–29). And in another letter to the same believers Paul confessed, "Therefore I will boast all the more gladly about my weaknesses, so that Christ's power may rest on me. That is why, for Christ's sake, I delight in weaknesses, in insults, in hardships, in persecutions, in difficulties. For when I am weak, then I am strong" (2 Cor. 12:9–10).

As you move toward *enough*—as you release your resources, live with less, and depend more on God—you will see a different level of anointing on your life. Desperation yields dependency, and dependency yields power. And as you decrease your earthly abilities through sacrifice and embracing less, you'll see your spiritual fruit increase. And suddenly we're back to "blessed are the poor in spirit . . ." (Matt. 5:3).

What do you have in your hand?

Fish and Bread

At the end of his Gospel, Luke shared an interesting story that wasn't recorded by any of the other Gospel writers. It's popularly known as the story of the walk to Emmaus. In Luke's account, Jesus appeared in his postresurrection form to two believers, one of whom was named Cleopas. We don't know the identity of the other person. Both seemed to have been followers of Jesus with close access to the original twelve disciples.

Jesus joined them as they were making the relatively short journey to the village of Emmaus. The two disciples failed to recognize Jesus and began describing to him the astounding events of the past forty-eight hours, including the resurrection of Christ as reported by Mary and her companions. When they reached the village, the two disciples invited Jesus to join them for supper. Luke then records, "When he was at the table with them, he took bread, gave thanks, broke it and began to give it to them. Then their eyes were opened and they recognized him, and he disappeared from their sight" (Luke 24:30–31).

There's something very significant about Jesus' actions that caused the disciples to recognize him. His pattern of taking, blessing, breaking, and then giving something away had divine authority behind it. We have no reason to believe that these two disciples were in the upper room for Jesus' final Passover meal with his original twelve disciples. Still, they would have seen this taking, blessing, breaking, and giving pattern before from Jesus.

On at least two occasions Jesus fed a multitude of several thousand people with just the meager provisions of a few fish and loaves of bread. The biblical writers are careful to record exactly what Jesus did before the miraculous feedings occurred:

- "And he directed the people to sit down on the grass. *Taking* the five loaves and the two fish and looking up to heaven, he *gave thanks* and *broke* the loaves. Then he *gave* them to the disciples, and the disciples gave them to the people" (Matt. 14:19).

- "Then he *took* the seven loaves and the fish, and when he had *given thanks*, he *broke* them and *gave* them to the disciples, and they in turn to the people" (Matt. 15:36).

- "*Taking* the five loaves and the two fish and looking up to heaven, he *gave thanks* and *broke* the loaves. Then he *gave* them to his disciples to set before the people" (Mark 6:41).

- "He told the crowd to sit down on the ground. When he had *taken* the seven loaves and *given thanks*, he *broke* them and *gave* them to his disciples to set before the people, and they did so" (Mark 8:6).

- "*Taking* the five loaves and the two fish and looking up to heaven, he *gave thanks* and *broke* them. Then he *gave* them to the disciples to set before the people" (Luke 9:16).

- "Jesus then *took* the loaves, *gave thanks*, and *distributed* to those who were seated as much as they wanted. He did the same with the fish" (John 6:11).

That's a very impressive biblical pattern. Why the repetition? Why the attention to detail? Why not just tell us that Jesus used a little food to feed a lot of people? Under the guidance of God's Spirit, the biblical writers obviously felt led to highlight the *taking*, *blessing*, *breaking*, and *giving* pattern. There's something very important to it. It shouldn't surprise us then that Jesus used the same pattern to reveal himself to the disciples in Emmaus.

In feeding the multitudes, there were always three results to the taking, blessing, breaking, and giving pattern. First, what Jesus took increased—I mean *really* increased. He took five loaves and two fish and fed over ten thousand people (five thousand Hebrew men plus their wives and children). That's serious multiplication. Second, the recipients were satisfied. There was no skimping here. God gave enough provision through Jesus for any and all who were hungry to be fed, not with just a little but until they were full. Third, they ended up with more than they had originally. A few loaves and fish became baskets of loaves and fish, even after everyone had eaten their fill.

No wonder the disciples remembered this pattern. No wonder they knew it to be divinely significant. Every time Jesus did his taking, blessing, breaking, and giving thing, good stuff happened. And so when those original disciples saw Jesus take the Passover bread, bless it in prayer, break it, and then give it to them, they must have known something was up. They wouldn't fully understand until after Jesus' resurrection, but they surely knew that Jesus' pattern wasn't random. He was telling them something.

Fish, Bread, Jesus, and You

The pattern of taking, blessing, breaking, and giving was exactly what God used in the life of Jesus. Perhaps that's why it was so important for Jesus to pass it on to his disciples. From eternity God had selected Jesus to become the Lamb that would remove the sins of the world. He was chosen (taken) before the first nanosecond of time ever ticked off. God anointed (blessed) Jesus with his own divine nature, and even went so far as to visibly and publicly bless him at his baptism. God broke Jesus through his suffering in those terrible hours before and during his execution. And then God multiplied Jesus' influence when he poured out his Spirit on all believers.

The results of the taking, blessing, breaking, and giving of Jesus are the same as well. Like the thousands for whom Jesus multiplied the fish and bread, we end up with more than we need. We can never drain dry the reservoir of God's holy provision for us through his Spirit. We will always have all that we need in him. Beyond that, we can drink of his Spirit until we are filled. He always satisfies. And when we grow weak, hungry, or thirsty again, we can return to him and be filled over and over.

But God's pattern of taking, blessing, breaking, and giving to meet others' needs didn't stop with Jesus. He does the same with and through us.

- *God takes us.* He wants you and all that you own. Like the bread and fish that the little boy gave, and like his Son who gave God everything, we are asked to fully give ourselves to God. He won't take us against our will; he will only take us when we invite him to. He wants you to willingly dedicate all that you are and have to his glory and kingdom purposes.
- *God sanctifies (blesses, declares holy) us and all that we own.* What God takes he blesses. Through the power of his Spirit, he is making you holy right now. But he

will also bless your possessions, your family, your time, your money, and your skills and gifts. Release all that you have to God and he will make it holy.

- *God breaks us.* Whatever God takes, he blesses and then he breaks it wide open. Jesus taught that unless a seed falls to the ground and dies, it can't produce life. But when it splits open in the ground, life comes out of it (see John 12:24). The same is true with us. Part of every believer's assignment is to receive the gift of brokenness that Jesus gives. It is only in our brokenness and emptiness that God can use us.

- *God gives us away.* God never gives us a blessing that he intends for us to keep. As he redeems us, as he gives us gifts and skills, as he blesses us with *more than enough*, he does so that he might meet the needs of others through us. Take a look in the mirror and then look around at everything you have—money, things, time, skills, education, experiences, passions, everything. And as you look at them, know that they aren't there for you. All you see (including yourself) is there for God to take, bless, break, and then give away.

When God gets through taking you, blessing you, breaking you, and then sharing you, the result will be exactly the same as when Jesus took the bread and fish. There will be more of you and your resources than when you started. The more of yourself and your resources that you give away, the more God will pour into you. Determine to be a funnel of resources and God will never stop pouring into you. You won't be able to give it away fast enough. He'll just keep pouring and pouring.

And when God gets through with you, others will be full.

Moving Toward Enough

From Heather: We started giving to the church every month, even when we couldn't pay our bills. I'm not sure if that's how it's supposed to work, but God has blessed our giving and we no longer have months where we come up financially short.

For Further Reflection

1. If God were to ask you what you have in your hands (resources, gifts, skills, time, education, passions, etc.), how would you answer him?
2. Read Matthew 26:26. When Jesus used the taking, blessing, breaking, and giving pattern as part of Holy Communion, what do you think he was trying to tell his disciples? What lesson did he want them to learn?
3. Reread Matthew 14:17–21. Every time you see a reference to the bread and fish (*them, fish, loaves*, etc.) substitute your name. Meditate on how the passage reads differently when you are what is being given away. Here's a guide to help you. Just insert your name:

> "We have here only _____," they answered. "Bring _____ here to me," he said. And he directed the people to sit down on the grass. Taking _____ and looking up to heaven, he gave thanks [for _____] and broke _____. Then he gave _____ to the disciples, and the disciples gave _____ to the people. They all ate [of _____] and were satisfied, and the disciples picked up twelve basketfuls of broken pieces [of _____] that were left over. The number of those who ate was about five thousand men, besides women and children.

16

"Less" Adventure

adventure (noun): a journey, an escapade, an exploit, a quest, an undertaking, or an exciting activity.[1]

We are designed to live by faith, not by sight. As Jesus' followers, we are intended to put our hope and trust in what we can't see, not in what we can see. The Scriptures teach that the just (the righteous, the redeemed, the saved) will live by faith.

If we're not extending ourselves, if we're not living in such a manner that requires faith, then we're not experiencing what God can and wants to do. We're not called to live irresponsibly but dependently. We need to live in a way that makes us desperate for God's provision. When we do, we can be certain that life will be a never-ending adventure.

What Will God Do This Time?

Susie and I have some dear friends in Austin. This man and his wife lead a vibrant church and often participate with me and other pastors in citywide events. At one such event, the funding we needed fell $10,000 short. My friend, who clearly has been given *more than enough* by God, stepped up and wrote a personal check to cover the difference.

My friend and his wife aren't millionaires, and I'm sure writing a check for $10,000 was a huge hit for them. But they demonstrated perfectly the kind of mind-set that *less* thinkers have. They saw a need, knew they had current provision to meet the need, and gave willingly. Their "right here, right now" mind-set turned into a blessing for thousands of people in Austin—believers and unbelievers—as the event they helped support was a huge success.

My friends also demonstrated another attribute of those who have learned to think *less*—expectation. As we discussed their gift over dinner recently, I affirmed my friends for their willingness to write the check that gave us the funding we needed. My friend didn't hesitate in his response: "We'll get it back." And then his wife added with a twinkle in her eye, "With a good measure, pressed down, shaken together and running over." Then they both just started laughing. It was like they were sharing an intimate secret.

What they were sharing, actually, was a biblical truth. With regard to generous giving Jesus once said, "Give, and it will be given to you. A good measure, pressed down, shaken together and running over, will be poured into your lap. For with the measure you use, it will be measured to you" (Luke 6:38). My friends seem to know that firsthand. They had obviously done such kingdom-minded investing before and had seen God-sized returns on their investments. Why should this time be any different? They know that when they step out in faith, God always comes through in exciting ways. All they have to do is sit back and see what God will do next.

And that is part of the adventure of living with less.

Crossing the Line

There really is a great sense of adventure that comes to those who have learned to think "less" and live with less. They have an ever-growing sense of awe and wonder at the amazing faithfulness and goodness of God. Now, I know that as you're reading this, "adventure" may not be what you're thinking about. You may be thinking, "Why would I want to live with less? Why would I want to deplete my rainy-day fund and run the chance of putting my family's provision at risk? That doesn't sound adventurous; it sounds irresponsible." I understand that thinking and still battle it myself sometimes. And if there ever existed a realm where God wasn't involved, such thinking would be reasonable to say the least.

But as Christians, we don't live in a realm without God. We live and move and have our being in the realm known as God's kingdom. We are citizens of his kingdom and children in his household. There is no chance of God not providing for us—none. So it's not irresponsible to seek the adventure that a life of faith brings; rather, it's normal. It's one of the things God wants us to experience as his children.

For you to see a life of less as an adventure instead of a source of fear and stress, you need to cross a line in your thinking in two critical areas. First, you need to know that God is good. In your core being you have to trust that God is righteous, holy, and a God of his word. You need to know that God has his kingdom best in store for you, even though his

217

plan for your life may be different from the one you'd write. Believing that God is good will help you close the debate on living with less and embrace the belief that moving toward *enough* really is a good idea.

Second, you need to know that God always comes through. You have to believe that God will keep his word and will give you what you need. It's a line of faith you must cross if you are going to have the courage to start living with less. Learn verses like Psalm 37:25, "I was young and now I am old, yet I have never seen the righteous forsaken or their children begging bread," and Hebrews 11:6, "And without faith it is impossible to please God, because anyone who comes to him must believe that he exists and that he rewards those who earnestly seek him." Reprogram your brain to lean toward the side of faith, not doubt. And then take some steps of faith. Do some things that will set you up to need and want the provision of God. He will come through for you. And when he does your faith will increase.

Once you determine that God is good and that he always comes through, you'll be well on your way to living the life of adventure that God desires for you. Like my two friends I mentioned in the previous section, you'll look for chances to step out in faith, increase your "less" by decreasing your "more," and put yourself in the position of wondering, not *if* God is going to come through, but simply *when* and *how*.

Jump

Part of the adventure of living with less is stepping out in faith and obedience without knowing the outcome. Consider Abraham, who left the security and favor of his hometown of Ur to follow God to a land he'd neither seen nor heard of before. Yes, such obedience seems scary at first. But once you come to trust in the goodness and provision of God, faith-based obedience becomes a source of sheer excitement, or as a friend and colleague of mine is fond of saying, *exhilarating terror*. Many of us are paralyzed by not knowing the outcome of our obedience. As a result, we often fail to step out.

In his book *Overcoming Buffaloes at Work and in Life*, Dr. Vincent Muli Wa Kituku writes:

> Over 80 percent of adults don't live up to their greatness be-cause they suffer from what I call "African Impala Syndrome." Jumping high and forward is an inborn talent for survival of the African impala. The impala is known to jump about ten feet high. This high jump propels the impala to land about thirty feet from the spot where it starts. With this ability of vertical and horizontal jumping, the impala survives and thrives in the carnivore-infested savannas of Africa.
>
> However, the impala has a unique limitation. It jumps only when it can see where it will land. I once read from an issue of "Bits and Pieces" that when the African impala is confined by a three-foot-high fence, it won't jump. As I think of the African impala, I often wonder how we fail to live up to our potential because we suffer from "African Impala Syndrome." We don't "jump" unless we can see "where we will land."[2]

The same is true for many believers. We know we're being called to jump into obedience and faith, but we hesitate be-cause we don't know where we'll land—we don't know how things will turn out. We're trapped by the fence of our own fears and disobedience. As a result, needs we could meet go unmet, our faith doesn't grow, and we miss the adventure of seeing God come through in immeasurable ways.

Exhibits A and Z

One of my kingdom heroes is George Mueller. If you need some inspiration to help you live with "less" and embrace the adventure that comes with it, then pick up one of the many biographies of Mueller's life. You'll never be the same. Let's call him Exhibit A.

Mueller ran a multipronged ministry for over forty years in Bristol, England, in the mid- to late-1800s. He pastored a church of 1,200 members, operated several Sunday schools that taught and evangelized thousands of children, and for decades he housed, fed, clothed, and educated thousands of orphans— sometimes up to 2,000 annually. Mueller also supported 187 missionaries, organized the Scriptural Knowledge Institute that distributed significant numbers of Bibles and gospel tracts. At the age of seventy he began a series of speaking tours that took him to Europe, Asia, North America, and Australia.

What makes Mueller so inspiring isn't just his work, but also the fact that in all those decades of ministry he never took a salary, never borrowed money, and refused to tell anyone but God about his needs. He would only pray about what he needed and trust that God would come through. Mueller's autobiography reads like an adventure novel, telling story after story of God's miraculous provision for himself, the two thousand orphans, and the rest of his work. During Mueller's forty-year ministry he "prayed in" the equivalent of millions of dollars of unsolicited donations. Then he gave most of it away.

When Mueller died in 1898, he was nearly penniless. He had chosen to keep almost nothing. But he had received more money through prayer alone than most of us will ever earn in our lifetimes. His legacy of faith and his testimony to God's faithfulness, as well as the ministry to orphans that he started, all carry on today. He is my Exhibit A of the provision and adventure that come to those who choose to live with less for the sake of others.

Austin Christian Fellowship is my Exhibit Z. I call us Exhibit Z because we're not even close to being in the same league as George Mueller. We are walking by faith as best we know how, and there is no doubt that we are seeing our share of God's provision and adventure.

In 2005 God led our church to start giving money away. At the same time he called us to become a "sending church"—to start sending teams of people to ministry around the world. I'm embarrassed to admit it, but we weren't a giving church. At the time, we were only giving away 1 percent of our annual receipts. On top of that, we had no missions sending ministry at all. We pretty much kept our money and our people to ourselves. After Hurricane Katrina hit, we saw the impact our giving and serving made on the people who had been forced to relocate to Austin because of the storm. We felt like it was time to start being more generous and to start walking by faith.

We determined through prayer to begin giving away significant amounts of money. We set a goal to eventually give away half of whatever we receive. We also determined to start sending ACF teams around the world as God would allow us. That was in 2005.

Today (I'm writing this in mid-2011), we invest 30 percent of our annual receipts in missions (this year's amount is $1.3 million). We give away 27 percent to ministries around the world and invest the remaining 3 percent in church planting here in the Austin area. We believe we'll be at 50 percent giving in the next three years. We also now send people regularly to Moscow, Uganda, Guatemala, Nicaragua, France, the US Gulf

Coast (for ongoing post-Katrina work), and we support over forty ministries here in Austin. Our mission opportunities are growing daily. In other words, once we decided to become a giving and sending church, our ministry impact exploded. God honored our obedience and opened countless doors for us.

He also led us into quite an adventure. We don't have the money in the bank that we've pledged to give away. There are ministries and families here in Austin and around the world counting on us to be part of God's provision for them. We've committed a certain amount to them, but we don't currently have that money. In order for us to honor our obligations, God has to come through. He always has. We've never missed a missions payment. Not once. In fact, we typically end up giving away more than we actually have budgeted. Watching God come through in so many different ways has been amazing and exhilarating.

Also, since 2005 we have practiced a discipline called vision-based budgeting. We use Jesus' feeding of the multitudes as our guide for how we budget. We ask our staff to pray about their visions for their respective ministries. We ask them, in the language of Scripture, to pray about what multitudes Jesus wants them to feed. We calculate the cost in assets and personnel that will be required to fulfill their respective visions, and then we budget accordingly. The projected annual expenses (our multitude that needs feeding) always significantly exceed our projected annual receipts (our loaves and fish). Then we pray like crazy and watch what God does. Needless to say, there are less stressful ways to create a budget. But we know that our hope doesn't lie in the stock market, the state of our nation's economy, or even the obedience of our people. Our hope is in God.

The fact that we give away so much of our receipts and that we budget in such a manner means that we rarely have much cash in the bank. We are a large church with a multimillion-dollar budget, but we rarely have more than $100,000 in the bank, and often it's significantly less. When we get money, we either give it away or spend it. We really do live by faith. Again, God has to come through.

On two different occasions in the past few years our operations director has come to me and told me we needed to start laying off staff. Now, this is not a man without faith. He loves God and believes his Word. But he also worked with a Fortune 500 business for almost two decades and knows when to start cutting losses. Based on the trends in giving and based on the best projections of the spreadsheets, we were set to run out of money in a matter of weeks or months. If we were to keep paying our bills and fulfill our mission obligations, then some staff would have to go.

And that's where the adventure part kicks in. When you know you're obeying God, when you know he has called you to live with less and trust him for what you don't have, then you get to sit back and see how God comes through. And that's what we did. (Okay, maybe we didn't really just sit back. Maybe we prayed like our lives depended on it!) In both cases I went to our elders and asked if they would support staying on our budget course and not cutting staff. They did. And in both cases we didn't let go of a single employee. We've never missed a payroll or had to let staff go because we couldn't afford to pay them. Not once. God has always come through.

Now several years into our faith-based living, we know we'd never go back to the old way of doing things. Yes, it's stressful. Yes, it requires constant prayer and time lingering over God's Word, reminding ourselves of his promises to be faithful. Yes, there are frequent weeks and months that are financially tight. But now we have a multiyear record of how God works. Now we have the data and history to prove that God comes through. Now we get to brag on God and tell how good he has been to us. We can point to our impact all over the world and know that God really did do it. There's no way we could have done any of this on our own, and there's no way we would have had such an impact if we had played it safe, limited our giving, kept our resources, and set budgets we knew we could make. Now playing it safe sounds downright boring. We'll never go back. The life of faith, the impact of releasing what God has given us, and the sheer exhilaration of seeing God come through are far too precious to give up.

What was true for George Mueller, what is true for our church, and what is true for countless other ministries and believers all over the world is true for you as well. If you'll live with less, release what you have, and depend on God for your provision, then your impact will explode, your joy will hit new, unimaginable levels, what God gives you to steward will increase exponentially, and your intimacy with Jesus will dramatically deepen.

Sounds like a no-brainer, right? What are you waiting for? Embrace "less."

Moving Toward Enough

From Jimmy and Jeannie: What have we gained? What's different?

His standard reigns in our home now, not our culture.

His Word reigns, not our understanding.

His love for us drives our actions, not desired love from others.

His presence lives in us and in our home, not preoccupation with our busy lives.

It's *his provision* we trust, not ours—no need to worry anymore.

It's *his heart* for the hurting beating in us, not our ideas of what people need.

It's *his Spirit* that drives who we talk to, approach, love, and mentor, not good deeds that try to make us feel valuable.

It's *his voice* we trust, not our own.

It's *his courage* freely given to us to follow, not our own.

It's *his calling* to be humble and live simply, not ours—no more hours spent on empty things.

It's *his kids* that live in our home for his purposes, not our kids.

It's *his house*, not ours.

It's *his freedom* we claim, not ours—no more bondage.

We're **his**, not our own.

Bottom line: Now we're a force to be reckoned with.

For Further Reflection

1. Have you ever given something away in faith, only to have God return it to you in a significant fashion? If so, what happened? If not, why not?

2. Read Genesis 12:1–3 and think about God's call of Abraham. What did and didn't God tell Abraham about his call? Think about what might have happened if Abraham had rejected God's call? Then think about what God is leading you to do and what the implications might be if you don't obey?

3. Think about a time when God led you to step out in faith without showing you how things would turn out. What happened? How did God come through for you and what did you learn?

Conclusion

The _____ Shall Inherit the Earth
(Fill in the blank: Powerful? Aggressive? Determined? Or
something else?)

There stood Abraham next to his nephew, Lot. He had a decision to make.

What would you have done?

Lot and his family had accompanied Uncle Abraham and Aunt Sarah when they left Ur to make their way toward Palestine. As they traveled together and began to settle in the land near Bethel, they quickly discovered that the land could not support both their families. Both Abraham and Lot were men of great resources, and each was traveling with a huge entourage and many herds of livestock. Their herdsmen began to fight over grazing and watering opportunities for their respective herds. Abraham's desire to help his nephew Lot was rapidly growing into a family feud.

Abraham then did a shocking thing. He offered to separate from Lot for both their sakes. As Lot's uncle, as the senior leader of the clan, and as the wealthier and more powerful of the two, Abraham could have ordered his nephew to go to a different region of Palestine. That, no doubt, was what Lot expected him to do. But Abraham didn't. He didn't flex his muscle or exercise his privilege. He deferred. He let Lot choose where he wanted to go.

What would you have done?

As Lot looked out at the landscape, he saw that there really was no choice. The land toward the Jordan River valley looked green, lush, and perfect for feeding and watering his flocks. Since his uncle had given him his pick, he chose the Jordan. That left the much less desirable, much more arid regions for Abraham. Abraham had clearly gotten the worse end of the deal. The two parted ways, and Lot and his horde moved into their plushy new digs.

What would you have done?

Not long after, the Lord spoke to Abraham. Here's the Genesis account of what he said: "Lift up your eyes from where you are and look north and south, east and west. All the land that you see I will give to you and your offspring forever. I will make your offspring like the dust of the earth, so that if anyone could count the dust, then your offspring could be counted. Go, walk through the length and breadth of the land, for I am giving it to you" (Gen. 13:14–17).

What a breathtaking scene. The opportunity that Abraham gave up, God gave back to him a hundredfold. It was as if God was just waiting for Abraham to release what he had so he could give him more than he could have ever gotten on his own. Abraham deferred and God honored it. Abraham sacrificed and God blessed him. Abraham waited and he received.

That's the principle of having more by living with less. If you grasp and grab and hoard, then you'll only have what you can hold, and eventually you'll probably lose that. But if you release, if you seek to honor others, if you serve others before you serve yourself, if you're a funnel for what God pours into you, then you will have more blessing, favor, influence, joy, and opportunities than you can ever achieve on your own.

What would you have done?

Nearly two thousand years after Abraham made his critical decision to release his rights and to live with less, Jesus summed up how God honors the "less is more" mindset with just a few words: "Blessed are the meek, for they will inherit the earth" (Matt. 5:5). In other words, it's not the aggressive, the pushy, or the greedy who inherit the earth (read, "have all they need"). Rather, it's the meek—the patient, the humble, and the generous. They, like Abraham, will not only get back what they let go of, they'll get it back in "good measure, shaken together and running over."

What will you do?

You can continue to push ahead, trying to achieve the elusive twins of security and satisfaction. Or you can move toward *enough.* You can take your *more than enough* and give part of it away, helping someone with *less than enough* move toward *enough.* You can strive or you can depend. You can achieve or you can receive. You can hoard or you can share. You can hang onto what you have, settle for the best you can do, and bless no one in the process. Or you can release what you have, bless countless others, and receive more than you could ever imagine.

What will you do?

Notes

Chapter 1 How Much Is Enough?

1. Amy Rosenberg, "Field Guide to the Materialist: She's Gotta Have It," *Psychology Today*, May/June 2007, http://www.psychologytoday.com/articles/pto-20070514-000006.html.

2. Paul Donsky, "Georgia Family Still Downsizing after $20,000 Gift," *The Atlanta Journal-Constitution*, Sunday, February 1, 2009, http://www.ajc.com/metro/content/metro/stories/2009/02/01/family_ebay_possessions.html.

Chapter 4 Perspective

1. Melanie Strick, *The Success Blog*, March 28, 2007, http://successconnections.blogspot.com/2007/03/wealth-statistics793-billionaires-in.html.

Chapter 5 Smog

1. Merriam-Webster Online, s.v. "smog," http://www.merriam-webster.com/dictionary/smog.

Chapter 6 Thorns

1. Merriam-Webster Online, s.v. "thorn," http://www.merriam-webster.com/dictionary/thorn.

Chapter 7 Barns

1. Merriam-Webster Online, s.v. "more," http://www.merriam-webster.com/dictionary/more.

2. Merriam-Webster Online, s.v. "barn," http://www.merriam-webster.com/dictionary/barn.

Chapter 8 Rich Man/Poor Man

1. According to 2009 statistics, the poverty line for single-parent homes with two children was an annual income of $17,285 or lower. See the US Bureau of the Census, *Income, Poverty, and Health Insurance Coverage in the United States: 2009*, Report P60, n. 238, p. 55, http://www.npc.umich.edu/poverty.

Chapter 9 What Does the Lord Require?

1. Merriam-Webster Online, s.v. "justice," http://www.merriam-webster.com/dictionary/justice.

Chapter 10 World-Class Christianity

1. Merriam-Webster Online, s.v. "world-class," http://www.merriam-webster.com/dictionary/world-class?show=0&t=1302640903.

2. Merriam-Webster Online, s.v. "sacrifice," http://www.merriam-webster.com/dictionary/sacrifice?show=1&t=1303145279.

3. For the whole amazing story, see Art Kabelowsky, "Out of Tragedy, Sportsmanship Has a Shining Moment," *Milwaukee Journal Sentinel*, February 16, 2009, http://www.jsonline.com/sports/preps/39694457.html.

4. For more on how to pray for yourself, see my book *Faith Set Free: Pray for Yourself with Reckless Abandon*.

Chapter 12 Birds and Bees

1. I'm defining tithing here as the giving of 10 percent or more of a person's annual gross income to a church or other Christian ministries. See http://library.generousgiving.org/page.asp?sec=28&page=223 and http://www.spiritrestoration.org/Church/Research%20and%20Polls/Tithing.htm for further details.

Chapter 16 "Less" Adventure

1. Merriam-Webster Online, s.v. "adventure," http://www.merriam-webster.com/dictionary/adventure.

2. Dr. Vincent Muli Wa Kituku, *Overcoming Buffaloes at Work and in Life* (Boise: Voice of Mukamba Press, 2008), 24.

Will Davis Jr. is the founding and senior pastor of Austin Christian Fellowship in Austin, Texas, and the author of several books, including the Pray Big series. Will and his wife, Susie, have three children. You can learn more about Will and follow his blog at www.willdavisjr.com. To download small group and devotional resources for *Enough*, go to willdavisjr.com/free-resources.

Meet Will Davis at
www.willdavisjr.com

Read his blog, listen to his messages,
and discover his books.

STAY CONNECTED ON
Pray Big willdavisjr

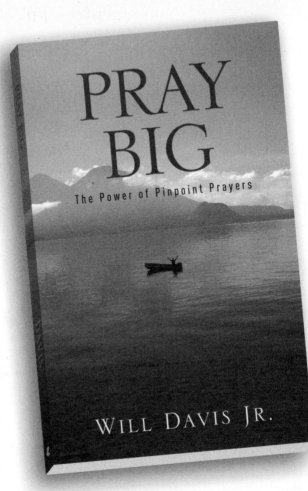

PRAY BIG

The Power of Pinpoint Prayers

WILL DAVIS JR.

"I am alive today because of the kind of bold praying you'll find in *Pray Big*. This important book can change your expectations about prayer, challenging you to seek God much more intimately, to ask for audacious requests more boldly, and to see big answers to prayer that change lives for eternity."

—Don Piper, bestselling author, *90 Minutes in Heaven*

BOLD, CONFIDENT PRAYER CAN MAKE ALL THE DIFFERENCE IN YOUR MARRIAGE AND IN YOUR FAMILY.

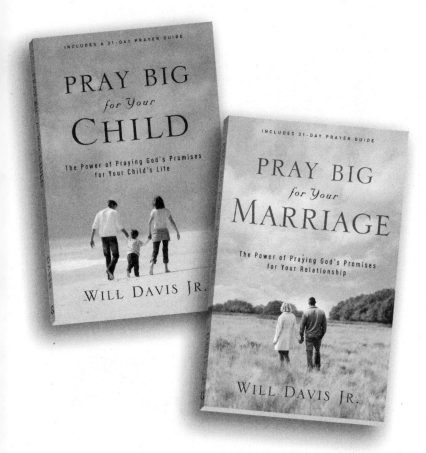

Visit www.willdavisjr.com

IT'S TIME TO **BANISH** THE **GUILT**.

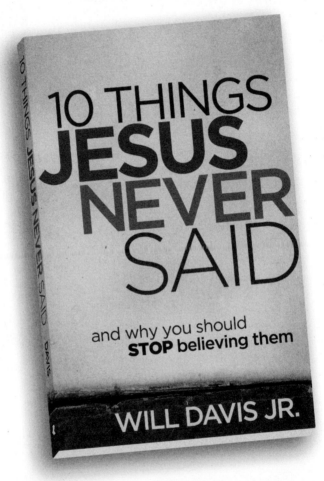

10 THINGS JESUS NEVER SAID

and why you should **STOP** believing them

WILL DAVIS JR.

If you've ever felt you didn't measure up to God's standards, it's time to stop believing the lies and start believing the things Jesus really did say.